America's Extraordinary Hotelman

STATLER

FLOYD MILLER

THE STATLER FOUNDATION, 250 PARK AVE., NEW YORK, N.Y.

Library of Congress Card Catalogue No. 68-20407
Cover and jacket design contributed by Needham & Grohmann.

Printed in the United States of America
By Cayuga Press, Ithaca, New York 14850

ACKNOWLEDGMENTS

By nature, biography is a joint venture – a partnership between the author and those men and women who knew his subject. Since Ellsworth Statler was of our time many former associates and employees are still living and have generously shared their memories with me.

My greatest debt is to E.M.'s widow, Alice Seidler Statler, who gave me long and uncomplaining hours. Such an exhuming of one she loved could not have been without pain, but she never flinched. Of great assistance were Ward Arbury and Peter Crotty, trustees of the Statler Foundation. They not only gave encouragement, but made available the Statler papers, scrapbooks, correspondence, office memos, company papers and bound volumes of "Statler Salesmanship."

Of assistance was Mrs. Frank McKowne, gracious and witty widow of Statler's righthand man. Company executives Harold B. Callis and D. B. (Bert) Stanbro withheld nothing of company politics. Peter Gust Economou, Buffalo's outstanding maitre d' and civic leader, recalled his boyhood days under Statler's aegis. Dr. Howard B. Meek, dean emeritus of Cornell's School of Hotel Administration, had pungent memories of the days when he was Statler's adversary as well as those when he was Statler's friend. Dean Robert A. Beck of the Cornell School offered me the School's facilities and hospitality during my research there. H. Victor Grohmann was a student during Statler's first angry invasion of Cornell's campus and made live for me a special facet of this remarkable and complex man. Anna Boyer, governess in the sometimes turbulent Statler household, was gentle and patient with both the past and me. The late James Rorimer, director of the Metropolitan Museum of Art, opened his family books and papers to reveal the close relationship between Statler and his father, Louis Rorimer. Harold Hatch did prodigious research for this volume and my debt to him is great.

The following friends and associates and employees of Statler's contributed their own memories and estimates, and they are the sinews of this book: Sam Abernethy, John A. Anderson, Charles Ashbaugh, Mrs. Leah Baylitts, Mrs. Glover Beardsley, Glover Beardsley, Frank Becht, Harry Beckwith, Alfred Benedette, Frank Bennett, Frank Boland, Clarence Boswell, Robert F. Brydle, John C. Burg, Walter J. Carney, Dan Catlin, Richard L. Collison, Charles Coyle, Tom Coyle, Francis Cunningham, Leonberger Davis, A. A. Demmer, William de Saussure, Arthur Dreher, Howard F. Dugan, Frank Duggan, C. K. (Copper) Dwinell, Jack Dyson.

Also Cecil Farrar, Thomas C. Farrington, Bernard Gimbel, William Greenhut, Walter Gregory, Edgar Hahn, Mrs. Martha Coppins Hamilton, James Henderson, Earl Hershberger, Ruth Hinkley, Phil Hummel, Edward (Ned) Humphrey, Dick Huntington, James Janis, James Keeshan, Elizabeth A. Kelly, Eugene Kelly, Paul T. Kilborn, Frank King, H. William Klare, Walter Kueffner, Martin Lammert, Gaston Lauryssen, George Lindholm, Mr. and Mrs. Leroy Linnard, A. H. (Tom) Longbotham, Vincent Lopez, Marty McAvoy, James H. McCabe, Thomas W. McQuaine.

Also Leo A. Molony, Frank J. Mathers, J. C. (Jack) Meacham, Dutch Miller, John Miller, J. D. Minster, Charles A. Moore, Harry Moorehouse, Frank E. Muenzel, Ed Murphy, Dr. J. Darwin Nagel, David Newton, George Pardoen, Tenton Parke, Karr Parker, John Peters, J. E. Pollock, Dr. W. F. Randolph, Frank A. Ready, W. B. (Buck) Reamer, Mrs. E. V. Renfrew, Lloyd Robinson, Malcolm Ross, James Ryan, Val Sanders, John Schantz, Edward Schlenker, Ida Schrage, Anthony Sestokes, Miss Daisy Shaw, Irving N. Simon, Michael Sperrazza, George Stark, Ernest G. Steck, Irene Steinberger, Arthur E. Surdam, Lenhard Thiele, Jesse Thurman, Thomas F. Troy, Earl H. Van Loon, Albert Vega, William Victor, William Walsh, Warren Welkes, Mrs. Elsie Wieland, John Woelfle.

I wish to thank Prof. Helen J. Recknagel and Mrs. Jane Reverand of *The Cornell Hotel & Restaurant Administration Quarterly* for their aid in the publication of this book.

FLOYD MILLER

FOREWORD

Ellsworth Milton Statler was an American business pioneer whose story has long needed telling. The greatness of America is the sum of the sweat and vision of such men as Ezra Cornell, George Eastman, Henry Ford, Thomas Watson, George Westinghouse, and, yes, Ellsworth Statler.

The hotel industry was vital to America's growth. Statler devised management techniques that were applicable far beyond the hotel business and contributed greatly to the nation's general efficiency. Nowhere was his inventiveness more apparent than in his sales effort and in his employee relations. To insure complete guest satisfaction he instructed his employees and he advertised to his guests that "The guest is always right!" He demanded peak performance from his workers and he received it — not only because he inspired loyalty but also because he was sensitive to their needs and aspirations. Statler's program of job and retirement security was unique in its time and has a vital message for management to this day.

Statler was a builder of men. Twenty years after his death in 1928, the hotels bearing his name were still all headed by men whom he had developed. Those men in turn passed his concepts on to younger men entering their employ. Today many hotel executives say with pride "I am Statler trained."

Statler's life has sometimes been referred to as a "Horatio Alger story." It is nothing of the kind. The Horatio Alger hero frequently sprang to success by means of a single heroic act or a stroke of luck. There were no such fortuitous events in Statler's life. Virtually without formal education he became a business giant, a multimillionaire, an intimate of the world's great, by will and industry and a flair for drama.

One of Statler's life ambitions was to open the road to success to succeeding generations through education. On the job he trained his employees well. Possessed himself of limited formal education, he placed a high value on such education and supported educational projects of all kinds. He was a principal contributor to the American Hotel Association's educational program of the early 1920's, especially the new hotel department organized largely at his instigation at Cornell University. Through the Statler Foundation, provided for in his will, his interest in education has been carried forward on a scale and in a manner he surely would have found most satisfying.

The imposing Statler Hall, home of the School of Hotel Administration on the Cornell campus, represents, together with other grants, a Statler investment of nearly $7,000,000. Other gifts and grants have been significant: $150,000 to New York City Community College for a Statler Wing; $125,000 to the City College of San Francisco for a Statler Wing; $122,500 to the American Hotel and Motel Association for its Educational Institute and other grants to the Association totaling $98,000 for research projects; and a total of more than $600,000 for scholarships distributed through hotel and motel associations throughout the United States and for a range of other types of assistance to many schools and colleges offering training for the hotel business.

The Statler story is an epic. Floyd Miller has told it with insight and suspense.

H. B. MEEK
Founder and Retired Dean
School of Hotel Administration
Cornell University
Ithaca, New York

STATLER – AMERICA'S EXTRAORDINARY HOTELMAN

"I WANT TO WORK HERE!"

Each morning for more than a year he had awakened before his brothers, tiptoed to the attic window and stared out across the Ohio River at the tallest building in Wheeling, West Virginia, the five-story McLure House. Before turning away he always made the declaration: "Someday I'm going there."

On this morning of August 12, 1876, the words came out differently. He heard himself saying, "Today I'm going there." He was startled and a little alarmed at the decision; it was as if someone else had made it for him, but once announced he had to carry it out. He was thirteen.

Late that afternoon he stepped off the ferry and began walking through the streets of Wheeling. He had been here before. With fleeting, urchin steps he and his friends had explored the town a number of times, but today was different. He was alone and he had come for something. He made directly for the McLure House.

When he finally stood before the hotel his courage gave way slightly. It was not the building which intimidated him so much as the men who entered and left it, who lounged in front of it, who paraded with such lordliness — the drummers.

They were a new breed of men created by the times. In the decades immediately following the Civil War the railroads extended their tracks thousands of miles and the river boats doubled in number, and doubled again. The traveling salesmen could now cover enormously expanded territories and wherever the trains and the boats took them, hotels were built to accommodate them.

Wheeling was served by both the Baltimore & Ohio Railroad and the packets that sailed the Ohio and Mississippi Rivers. She was the gateway to the west and south, and through her portals marched thousands of drummers who stopped briefly at the prosperous McLure House.

The boy thought he had never seen anything so grand as these men with the fleshy pink faces and the easy laughter. The brims of the derby hats were curled tighter, their shoes squeezed narrower, their jacket shoulders padded wider than ordinary men's. Their stiff-bosomed shirts were decorated with sprigs of violets, and their vests gave breathtaking display to stripes or polka dots or cascading waves. It was difficult to believe that men so caparisoned could deal with such mundane things as pins and washboards and horsecollars.

After several minutes of awed admiration, the boy moved through them and into the hotel. He knew he wanted to go to the front desk and he spotted it on the far side of the lobby. As he drew near he saw that the desk clerk was busy with two very important-looking men and he dared not intrude. His steps slowed and finally came to a halt in the middle of the vast room. He looked around in wonder. The place had been described to him but reality beggared the words.

The floor of the lobby was of marble, and scattered over it were groupings of heavy oaken chairs and tables, each served by an enormous spittoon polished to a golden glitter. The walls were laced with oak beams cut into Gothic arches and dripping with wooden pendants. From one wall the head of a passive mountain goat looked down with glassy eyes; from another a buffalo had his lips twisted in a fierce snarl put there by an imaginative taxidermist; and on a third wall a giant sailfish arched its back in a leap that never ended.

Beneath the fish was the front desk which held a ledger in which the guests registered, an inkwell cradled in the arms of two tiny brass maidens naked to the waist, and a cup full of shot into which was thrust a pen. Behind the desk, rows of hooks held the room keys, simple skeleton keys to which were attached large wooden blocks meant to discourage the guests from absent-mindedly putting the keys in their pockets when leaving town.

Flanking the desk were archways leading to other public rooms. To the left was the billiard room, hazy with cigar smoke and punctuated with the dry click of ivory balls striking each other. In this room the conversation was intermittent, murmurous with concentration. Not so the room glimpsed through the other arch; there the conversation was boisterous and broken by laughter and bits of song. This was the barroom, shimmering with mirrors and crystal and polished wood and emitting a comforting, yeasty odor.

By the time the boy had completed his examination of the lobby, the important-looking men had departed from the desk and the clerk was now concentrating on some paperwork. He was a lad of twenty and he wore, he was firmly convinced, the widest and most beribboned sleeve garters in town. Though pretending not to be, he was well aware of the boy in threadbare clothes whose straight blond hair was cut in random scallops and ridges.

The clerk felt it beneath his dignity to speak to the boy, but on the other hand the presence of so shabby a creature in the lobby was an insult and should be disposed of. Since ignoring him did not seem to accomplish banishment, he was forced to speak.

"Boy," he called out, "what do you want?"

Approaching the desk, the boy said, "I've come for a job."

The clerk gave a knowing wink to some drummers standing nearby and said, "Oh? As manager?"

"No, sir," the boy replied soberly, "as a bellboy."

Having won no laughter from the drummers on his previous thrust, the clerk dropped his bantering tone and said coldly, "We have all the bellboys we need." He returned his attention to the ledger, thus dismissing the applicant. The boy refused to accept dismissal.

"Yes, sir," he said, "I know that. But my brother Charlie says that sometimes some of them don't show up on the night shift and you're shorthanded."

"Oh, your brother Charlie said that, did he? And who the hell is he?"

"He's a bellboy here. Charlie Statler."

"There are no jobs open and I don't think there is gonna be any. *Unless* your brother Charlie gets too lippy. Now on your way. We don't want kids hanging around the lobby."

Twenty-four hours later, at exactly 6 p.m., the desk clerk looked up to find the same boy standing in the same spot. "Now look, kid . . . ah, what's your name?"

"Ellsworth."

"Now look, Ellsworth, I told you there were no jobs. . ."

"That was last night. There might be one tonight."

"Well, there isn't!"

"I'll be back tomorrow night," the boy said.

And he was. Even the clerk began to feel grudging admiration for his cheerful persistence. "How old are you, kid?" he asked.

"Thirteen."

"You're a little young to work a hotel. My advice is to look for another job."

"Oh, I got a job all right, but I want to work here.

"What kind of a job do you have?"

"I stoke the glory hole in LaBelle glassworks over in Kirkwood."

The clerk looked at him with disbelief. "Stoking the glory hole . . . at thirteen?"

"Been doin' it for four years," the boy said.

Grudgingly, the clerk looked at the boy with respect. He knew that stoking the glory hole was one of the roughest jobs in the glass factory. To take such a job at nine... well, only a desperately poor family would allow such a thing.

The Statler family was poor, certainly, but going to work had been more the boy's decision than the parents'. Ellsworth Milton Statler was strong-willed, even at nine.

CHAPTER 2

THE FAMILY

Poverty is less apparent in a large family than in a small one. The mere quantity of equipment needed to dress, feed and house eleven people tends to mask any privation. Eleven chairs around a dinner table, no matter how battered, make an impressive sight; and if the meal consists of nothing more than porridge, eleven bowls of the stuff is formidable.

Moreover, the Statler family had little leisure in which to be conscious of their poor estate. Mary Statler lost two children at birth, but raised nine: Charles, Lillian, Govinda, Elizabeth, Alabama, William, John, Ellsworth and Osceola. Her husband, William Jackson Statler, was a part-time preacher and since he was convinced that beautiful rewards awaited him in heaven he had little interest in acquiring temporal possessions.

William was a German immigrant who came to Somerset County in Pennsylvania in the spring of 1850, met and married a soft-spoken Scotch-Irish girl named Mary Ann McKinney. He became pastor of the German Reformed Church near Gettysburg and his farmer congregation was as poor as he. As the children began to arrive at regular intervals it became clear, even to William, that he could not support his family on the meager collections taken each Sunday at church. He began to think about the problem.

He was a ponderous man with heavy features and blunt fingers, and he never made an impulsive decision. In the third winter of his marriage, with Charles and Lillian al-

6

ready born and Govinda on her way, he borrowed a set of encyclopedia and began methodically to study it. He started at the beginning, at A, and worked his way through the alphabet. Sometimes he skimmed the pages, sometimes he carefully studied the words. His wife had no idea what he was searching for and he did not tell her. In truth, he did not know himself, but he was convinced that when he found the proper thing he would recognize it. In the sixth month of his study he found it. It was in the volume marked M.

He read the page several times, frowning in concentration, then pushed the book away from him and turned to his wife.

"Mary, what is it that every farmer needs?"

"Why, I . . . I don't know, William."

"Put your mind to it, woman," he said with some annoyance.

She frowned, hoping that by wrinkling her forehead she would produce the answer he desired. "Seed?" she finally said.

"Of course he has to have seed and fertilizer too. But that's not what I mean. What is it he *can* get along without but doesn't want to. A sort of necessary luxury, you might say." He gave her several moments to come up with the answer, then said triumphantly, "Matches!"

"Matches?"

"Of course . . . Of course! In the winter he can always take an ember out of the stove, but what about in the summertime when the stove isn't burning? He needs matches. You won't find a farm from here to Lancaster that doesn't need matches."

"I guess you're right, dear," she said, using the words with which she always met his proclamations.

"Well, I know how to make matches." He tapped a finger on the volume marked M. "It's all here in this book. Let me read it to you." He picked up the book and read:

"Wood splinters are dipped in a mixture of yellow phosphorus, chlorate of potash, red lead, nitrate of lead, and peroxide of manganese." He dropped the book back on the table and said, "I can get the chemicals from the drug store in town, shouldn't cost much, and wood splinters won't cost me nothing. I can make the matches right here in our own kitchen and then take them out and sell them to the farmers for five cents a package."

"Won't it be dangerous?" she asked.

"Not when you know what you're doing."

Over the following months the Statler kitchen was filled with acrid fumes. The Reverend Statler might preach on Sunday about hell's fire and brimstone in the afterworld, but during the week he and his family experienced it in their own kitchen. By some miracle there were no explosions and the inventory of match packets slowly grew. By spring he had several hundred of them and was ready for business. He hired a horse and buggy from a livery stable at the reduced "preacher's rate" and one morning at dawn took off into the countryside. That evening he returned home in a state of exhilaration.

"I been at the Steurman farm. Had a long talk with Gunther Steurman and I think he now sees the light. He's been deep in the sin of disbelief, a prideful man, a blasphemer, but all that is now changed. He's asked the Lord's forgiveness. I've saved a soul, Mary."

They sat down to the evening meal and were halfway through it before Mary asked, "Did Gunther Steurman buy any matches?"

The question seemed to surprise her husband and he thought on it for a moment. Then he smiled. "Oh, yes, he bought a pack."

"Who else did you sell to?"

"Who else? Nobody else. I told you I spent the day at the Steurman farm."

"One pack of matches doesn't even pay for the hire of

the rig." She spoke softly, without reproach, merely making an observation of fact.

He scowled, genuinely shocked by the implication of her words. He said to her, "Which is more important, spreading God's Word or selling matches?"

There could be only one answer to that question, of course. She gave him a gentle smile, reached across the table to pat his hand. She knew she had married a man who was good but impractical. She did not regret it, for she had the conviction that God would somehow take care of them. And He did, somehow.

For the next several years William made and peddled matches through the countryside, and while it proved a most effective way of finding lost souls and sinners, it didn't solve the problem of feeding a family that every nine months increased by one. At last William was forced to take direct action; he became a farmer. That is to say, he planted a truck garden and gave it what attention he could between the more pressing duties of preacher and match salesman.

Mary was carrying her tenth child when, on the opening days of July 1863, she heard the cannonading of the battle of Gettysburg just a few miles to the west. While she was skeptical about the theory of prenatal influences, she thought it well to take steps to counter whatever effect the sounds of war might have upon the unborn child. A major part of her meager dowry had been a twelve-volume set of Milton's *Paradise Lost*, and she now began reading aloud from it, her voice rising above the sounds of battle.

> What in me is dark
> Illumine, what is low raise and support;
> That to the height of this great argument
> I may assert eternal Providence,
> And justify the ways of God to men.

The battle passed into history, and where there had been death, birth began again. On October 26, 1863, Mary's baby was born. It was a boy and she gave him a name of deep symbolism: Ellsworth Milton Statler. The Ellsworth was for the dashing Col. Elmer Ellsworth, an intimate of President Lincoln and commander of an elite Union regiment of New York City firemen who wore special uniforms with red pants and called themselves Zouaves. The name Milton was, of course, for the blind English poet whose work she had read during pregnancy.

She was hedging her bets. If the child was to be influenced by the sound of cannon, let him not be an ordinary soldier, but a hero. On the other hand, if the poetry was to shape him, let him be as wise and moral as Milton.

None of her other children had received such portentous names; did she have a premonition about this child? Did she see in the small red face at her breast something more than she had seen in the nine preceding faces? Perhaps so, for within a few short years it became clear that this child was quite different from his brothers and sisters. He was to become neither a soldier hero nor poet, but he was to leave his mark on America.

The Reverend William Statler was a railroad buff. Being a poor man he could not ride in them, but his vicarious pleasure was intense. Whenever possible he arranged his match selling itinerary so that he was beside a stretch of track when a train was scheduled to pass by. He'd climb down from the buggy, securely hitch the horse, then patiently wait for the show.

In the silent country air the tracks could be heard humming before the train appeared over the horizon. Down the gleaming rails and at the distant point where they merged into one, an antlike thing would appear. It began to puff itself larger and larger until the smokestack took form. It was a towering funnel-shaped affair that seemed larger than the engine itself, and out of it poured a cloud of smoke flaked through with white bits of wood ash.

The apparition rocketed toward William at a full thirty miles an hour, and with each passing moment it grew larger and noisier. The brass kerosene lantern could soon be seen and it had a lens larger than a man's head. Below it the cow-catcher thrust its iron ribs forward to sweep the track clear of obstructions.

A puff of purest white appeared above the engine, and moments later a whistle echoed through the hills. The engine came opposite William, filling his ears with roar and clatter and a dragonlike hissing. Past his eyes there streaked a smear of vermilion from the spinning wheels. The engine, smelling of iron and warm oil, gave way to the wooden passenger cars that groaned in protest at the speed being forced upon them. There was a quick blur of faces peering out the narrow, romanesque windows, and then the train had passed.

William looked after it, watched it shrink. Again there appeared the puff of white steam, and again the whistle rolled over the countryside. William thought there was no sound on earth quite so hauntingly pure and beautiful and, for a reason he could not understand, melancholy. He would not allow envy in his heart, but he couldn't help reaching the conclusion that people who rode trains were favored above their fellow men.

He wondered vaguely about railroads in heaven. He even wrote a hymn about them and no Sunday service ever ended without his leading his flock in full-throated rendition of "The Spiritual Railway."

> The way to heaven by Christ was made,
> With heavenly truth the rails were laid,
> From earth to heaven the line extends,
> To life eternal where it ends.
>
> Repentance, faith, the stations where
> Passengers are taken in.
> No fare is there for them to pay
> For Jesus is himself the way.

The Bible is the engineer.
It points the way to heaven so clear.
Through tumults dark and dreary here,
It does the way to glory steer.

God's love the fire, His truth the steam
That drives the engine and the train.
All you who would to glory ride
Must come to Christ, in Him abide.

The secret closet is the place,
The water station of His Grace.
We there receive and run so fast
To gain a home in heaven at last.

Come then, poor sinners, now's the time
At any station on the line.
If you repent and turn from sin,
The train will stop and take you in.

The parishioners ultimately grew tired of "The Spiritual Railway," but their pastor ignored all hints that the hymn be given a respite and each Sunday boomed it out with undiminished vigor.

CHAPTER 3

MOVE TO BRIDGEPORT

"I hear land is going real cheap out west," William said to his wife one evening. He spoke with such elaborate casualness that his wife knew immediately it was a matter of some importance to him.

"That so?" she said neutrally.

"Lots of folk are moving out there. Good folk, with get-up-and-go. Gonna be boom times, they say."

"Where is all this happening, William?"

"Oh, lots of places out there." He waved his hand. "Talked to a fellow today who says Wheeling is a good place. Right on the Ohio River, steamboats making it a real busy port. Gonna grow fast," he said.

There was a moment of silence while he waited for her to question him, to make it easier for him to say what he had to say. But she refused to help. She was a loyal wife and she would move with him whenever and wherever he determined, but she would not make it easy for him. He would have to say the words himself.

He finally cleared his throat and said, "I been figuring things. We could sell our place here for enough to set us up out there."

"On how many acres?" she asked, thinking of their meager harvest.

"I wasn't thinking about farm acreage, Mary. Considering the way that area is bound to grow, might be a good idea to set up a store, go into business."

It seemed to her that business was the least of his tal-

13

ents. Certainly his experience with the matches would indicate so.

"Do you think you could get a pulpit out there?" she asked.

"A man doesn't need a pulpit to spread God's Word," he said with some heat. "Personal and individual counselling is often more effective."

She nodded thoughtfully. "We'd have to buy a horse and wagon to get there," she said.

"That won't be necessary. The railroad runs all the way to Wheeling."

She looked at him quickly but he avoided her eyes. Was he uprooting his family and moving them west so that he might at last satisfy his ambition to ride a train? Certainly it was a factor in his decision, but how big a one she didn't know. Nor, perhaps, did her husband. One thing was perfectly clear, however. Whatever their new life, it couldn't be more difficult than the present one. There was really no reason not to go.

The two-hundred-mile train ride was every bit as glorious as William thought it would be. Rocketing over the hills and through the valleys of western Pennsylvania at thirty-five miles an hour gave him thrills he would never forget. There was one disappointment, but he tried to put it aside and not let it spoil the pleasure of the trip. He had introduced himself to the engineer and identified himself as a preacher. He let it be known that he would be mighty obliged to receive an invitation to ride a spell in the cab of the engine. But the invitation never came.

The Statler family settled, not in Wheeling but across the river in the small Ohio village of Bridgeport where William found a business for sale. A two-story wooden structure contained a general store on the first floor and living quarters on the second. It was exactly what he had hoped to find, and he considered the discovery providential. Had he been a more sophisticated man he would have been warned by the alacrity with which the owner agreed to sell. Had he been experienced in commerce he would have investigated the business climate of the village. Convinced that God had led him here, he felt that such precautions were not only unnecessary but perhaps even blasphemous. William Statler forever overestimated God's interest in the details of his life.

A dormitory of double-decker bunks was built in the attic for the sons, the daughters slept on the second floor, the parents in the rear of the store. The store itself was a long and gloomy cavern lined with shelves that held molasses, vinegar, coffee, rubber boots, kerosene, calico cloth, licorice, fly swatters, brooms, seed potatoes, axle grease, pickles, axe handles, thread, canvas gloves and patent medicines. Since there was little ventilation each item contributed its own odor to the total pungency which, though not unpleasant, was penetrating. After a time the Statler family carried the aroma of their trade with them wherever they went.

Toward the rear of the store there was a potbellied stove. It provided heat, of course, but more important was its traditional role of marking the place of the village forum. Any man with fifteen minutes to spare, or an hour, or a day, habitually came here to hitch up a chair, use the pan of ashes as a spittoon, and deliver his opinion on great and small events. William had no objection to this custom; in fact, he welcomed it for he saw here a congregation of souls to be saved.

The men of Bridgeport were ready enough to discuss religion but in moderation, not to the exclusion of all temporal matters. And they didn't want to be preached at with such a joyless doctrine as that held by William Statler. They didn't feel that their sins were of such dimension as to earn the fire and brimstone William promised them.

One by one the men stopped coming and within a

month the stove had no function to perform save that narrow one for which it was originally designed.

When the men of the village had gathered around the stove each day there had been created an illusion of commerce, but with them gone it became painfully clear how few paying customers entered the front door. Bridgeport was deep in a post-Civil War depression and even if William Statler had possessed a more generous and attractive personality it was unlikely that he could have made anywhere near an adequate living out of the store. The winter of 1869 was a bad one.

The children entered school and for a few brief hours each day they were able to forget the bleakness of their lives at home. Immediately after school, however, they were expected to hunt for coal. The land surrounding Bridgeport was scarred by strip mining where the coal veins were close enough to the surface to dig up without the cost of sinking shafts. Around these open mines were ugly mounds of slag, discarded coal of such poor quality as to be unmarketable. It *would* burn if almost constantly tended, and it was free for the taking. Every day after school the Statler children could be seen on the slag heaps filling gunny sacks and dragging them home.

The family staggered on, month after month, and if they weren't really starving the fear of it constantly shadowed their lives.

In the summer of 1872 good news spread through the village — a factory was coming to the area. The LaBelle Glass Factory was to locate in Kirkwood, Ohio, which was within walking distance of Bridgeport. The skilled glass blowers would be brought in from other parts of the country, but there would be unskilled jobs for children. The jobs would pay fifty cents a day.

The two older boys, Charles thirteen and William eleven, applied for jobs and got them. That evening Ellsworth announced that he too wished to go to work at the glassworks. Mary Statler had found it difficult enough to accept the fact that her two older boys were quitting school and she was dead set against the factory making any more inroads on her family.

"Ma, I've had two winters of school," Ellsworth said. "I can read and write."

"That's not enough," she said. "I want you to know arithmetic, and history, and . . ." She had run out of subjects and she made a sweeping gesture with her hand. "I want you to know about the world. No, Ellsworth, you must go back to school at least until you're William's age."

The father remained silent during this exchange, and Mary realized she could not count on his support. He wouldn't actively support his son, either, for he found no principles involved on either side. He was a man unsuited to the world and therefore found the world unsuitable. Over the past year he had retreated more and more into himself where he was engaged in preparation for heaven. He saw very clearly the flutter of white wings above golden streets, he heard the celestial music, and he could not bring his attention back to the slag heaps and factories of Bridgeport.

The contest over school was between mother and son. And she lost it.

She understood Ellsworth the least of any of her children. He was a quiet boy who caused no trouble in the family except for an almost maddening stubbornness. Once he had decided upon some course of action, he did it. He had decided to go to work in the glass factory and his will was stronger than his mother's.

On the first day of work Charles and William and Ellsworth set out for the glassworks. Ellsworth had almost to trot on his short, stocky legs to keep up with his older brothers. He was nine.

CHAPTER 4

"GLORY HOLE"

The LaBelle glassworks was an ugly pile of native stone that stood close to the west bank of the Ohio River. The windows were mere slits in the masonry and afforded the interior little light and no ventilation. That the place was offensive to the eye and depressing to the spirit seemed entirely proper to the community, for no one expected a factory to have any felicity of architecture. It was a place where men worked, and no one was expected to enjoy work, only to be grateful for it.

While the outside of the structure was grey and mean, the great workroom inside was lurid with fire and acrid with the smell of roasting chemicals. Orange flames leaped in a dozen furnace pots, sending forth blistering heat and making grotesque shadows dance like souls in torment. It seemed a pit of hell, and it brutalized the men who worked there.

The foreman's name was Andy Boggs and on the first day he looked down at the three Statler children with a habitual expression of distaste. "You each get a glory hole to fire," he said. "Ya work for the snapper-up and ya do what he tells ya. And ya do it goddamn fast if ya don't wanna get kicked." He studied the smallest boy. "What's yer name, kid?"

"Ellsworth," came the answer.

"Ellsworth! Jesus, whoever give ya that handle? How old are ya?"

"Nine."

"Kinda small for yer age, ain't ya?"

18

"I can do the work."

The calm reply annoyed the foreman and he growled, "We don't want any smart alecks here, and no horseplay on the job. You get paid twenty-five cents a turn, which is six hours. You can work two turns a day for fifty cents. Ya got that straight?"

The boys solemnly nodded.

"Come on, then, and I'll show ya what ya gotta do."

They entered the great workroom and the boys saw for the first time the fire and the shadows, and their hearts skipped a beat. Boggs noticed their brief moment of hesitation and he said, not unkindly, "Do your jobs right and ya won't get hurt." His statement was not entirely true, as he well knew.

In the center of the room was the main fire that roared in an oven made of brick and shaped in a round dome. Opening out of the perimeter of the dome were twelve smaller and individually fired ovens in which nestled the pots holding the molten glass. Near each of these furnaces there was a still smaller furnace named the "glory hole" and used to heat and soften glass pieces after they had been given their first form and before being delivered into the hands of the finishers. These glory holes, fired by coal, were to be tended by the boys.

Around the walls of the workroom were bins holding fuel, white sand, lime and soda ash. The sand and chemicals were mixed in large troughs, then trundled to the pots for melting, 2,500 pounds of it for each firing. After the mixture had cooked for twenty-four hours it was ready to be worked. The "snapper up" (a man who "snapped up" the molten glass out of the fire with a long rod called a punty) now approached the pot and took a sample of the molten glass to see if it was ready for working. If it was, he inserted the punty into the mixture, gave it a series of deft whirls to collect a ball of the glass, then carried it to the "presser." The presser was a man who operated a press mould into which was poured the viscous glass. With a quick slam of the presser's foot on a treadle, the mould closed hard and forced the glass into the shape of a goblet or a bottle or whatever was being made.

The press was opened after a moment and the goblet lifted out with a forked stick and carried to the glory hole for reheating. When again hot enough for working, the glass was finally delivered to the finisher who placed it on a spinning table and, using water-soaked sugarwood paddles, shaped and smoothed the goblet into its permanent form.

The workers moved with grace and skill to handle the glowing glass of many colors, jewel greens, ruby reds, soft lavenders. Such precision of timing was required that the movements of the workers became stylized, resembling a ballet, but the truth was it was hot, dangerous, brutal work.

Andy Boggs took Ellsworth to one of the glory holes where a hulking man with dirty red hair leaned on a punty.

"Rube, I got you a boy," the foreman said.

The man named Rube turned small, bloodshot eyes on the boy. After a moment of study he said, "Ain't hardly weaned."

"He says he can do the work. His name is Ellsworth."

"Ellsworth!" Rube cried. "Ellsworth! Jee-zuzz!"

"He says he can do the work," Boggs repeated. "Ya want him or not?"

Rube shrugged his massive shoulders. "If you got nothin' better." He punctuated this sentence with a spit of tobacco that landed between the boy's feet. "Don't stand there all day," he roared at the boy. "Fire up the glory hole."

Ellsworth turned and ran to the coal bin and began to shovel the fuel into a wheelbarrow. When it was full he reached for the handles and lifted, but nothing happened. The wheelbarrow seemed riveted to the floor. The trouble was that the handles of the barrow were too far apart for his short arms. He could just reach them, and thus had little leverage for lifting. He tried again and the back legs of the barrow just barely lifted from the floor, but sufficient for him to start forward with a rush.

The barrow traveled a straight line for about ten feet, then began to veer to the left. The boy tried desperately to straighten it out, but it had tilted, shifting the center of gravity, and he had not the strength to right it. At the last moment, just as the barrow was about to go over, spilling its load of coal, the boy dropped the handles and let the barrow come to a shuddering stop . . . upright. Rube, his snapper-up, had watched the performance from a distance, a mocking expression on his face.

The boy grabbed up the barrow for a fresh start and this time was able to complete the trip to the glory hole. He unloaded the coal into the fire and returned to the bin. He knew he could not safely wheel a full load, so this time he filled the barrow only half-full and made the trip without incident. This limitation on load size meant he would have to make twice as many trips as the other boys, and twice as fast. He determined to do it.

After completing the fourth trip he paused for a moment to stare at the glory hole's orange flames. Immediately something struck him, sending him sprawling to the floor. He saw nothing but blackness and stars, but then his vision cleared and he looked up into Rube's face flushed with anger.

"What the hell you think you doin'?" he stormed, "watchin' a sunset? Get that coal movin'!"

Ellsworth scrambled to his feet and raced the wheelbarrow back to the bin. He found that he was shaking with his own anger and resentment. He thought himself unlucky to have Rube for his boss, but by the end of the day he learned that he was actually fortunate. The other snapper-ups had a habit of kicking their glory hole boys on the shins. This was a tradition in the glassworks, a method of discipline the snapper-up workmen considered their right. The human shin is a surprisingly tender part of the body when kicked with a hard shoe, and the boys would scream in agony and dance on one leg.

"But," explained Andy Boggs, "it keeps 'em moving. We got no loafers in this plant."

Serious and sometimes lasting injury was done to the children. The blood vessels were often crushed, causing varicose veins, sometimes gangrene, and even amputations. Years later, any man who walked the streets of Bridgeport with a limp was immediately recognized as having once been a glory hole boy in the glassworks. Ellsworth Statler was lucky to have been assigned to Rube who was, for some reason, a hitter instead of a kicker.

When the three Statler brothers returned home after the first day's work their mother ran to them with anguished cries. They were covered with coal dust, had blistered hands, and her youngest had a bruised face as well. She cleaned them and comforted them and fed them, and all the time was puzzled by their attitudes. They didn't complain or cry, they boasted. They had been through a hellish day and survived. They felt like men.

In the middle of the night Ellsworth awoke to hear his mother softly weeping. He knew she wept for him and he wished he could make her understand how things were with him. He *wanted* to work in the factory rather than go to school. He would rather learn how a ruby red goblet was made than read about something that happened one hundred years ago. He had an intense curiosity about his own world.

He heard his father speak to his mother. The voice was slow and rhythmic, his pulpit voice, his praying voice. Lately, that was the only voice he used. The most commonplace observations were announced in dolorous cadences, as if the words carried a divine significance. Now, in the middle of the night, he was telling his wife that she should not weep over the fact that her three sons had to quit school and go to work, for it was God's will. This being the case, to weep was a form of blasphemy. The weeping continued, nevertheless. It was doubtful that Mary Statler even heard her husband. She had lost the habit of listening to him.

CHAPTER 5

PIONEER WHEELING

There was no one in the glassworks, man or boy, who did not feel the lure of the town across the river — Wheeling.

She was a growing, strutting, busting, rootin'-tootin' town of 50,000 people. Her iron foundries made more stoves than any other city in the country; her wagon factory turned out carriages of great style; her lantern factory supplied farms and barns throughout the entire Mid-West with nighttime illumination; sixty percent of the nation's consumption of iron nails were made in Wheeling. Also, Wheeling had more saloons and sporting houses per population than any town in the country.

Geography was largely responsible. Just before the Civil War the B & O Railroad had extended its tracks to Wheeling in order to meet up with the river boats that sailed down the Ohio and the Mississippi Rivers all the way to the Gulf. The town became a transportation hub through which flowed both freight and travelers. At about the time the railroad drove its final track spike, the enterprising McLure family completed its hotel, built on the gamble that growth and prosperity were coming to town.

The five-story McLure House opened in 1852 and became one of the outstanding hotels of the post-Civil War era, in the same class as the Monongahela in Pittsburgh, the American House in Philadelphia, and the Tremont House in Boston. As Harry, Frank and Bernie McLure had hoped,

24

E. M. STATLER'S
MATERNAL
GRANDPARENTS
AND HIS MOTHER,
SHOWN HOLDING
ONE OF HIS
BROTHERS.

Ellsworth Milton Statler's mother, of Scotch-Irish descent, was Mary Ann McKinney before her marriage to Rev. William Jackson Statler in 1850. Mrs. Statler inherited her features from her father. Young Ellsworth, her tenth child, resembled his mother. Photographs were developed from early daguerreotypes.

HOTEL McLURE

About 1869, the Statlers moved from a farm near Gettysburg (Pa.), where Ellsworth had been born in October 1863, to Bridgeport (Ohio), shown as the village across the river from Wheeling (W. Va.) in the photograph to the upper left. At nine, Ellsworth worked in a Bridgeport glass factory, lugging buckets of coal. When he was thirteen, he crossed the bridge to Wheeling's leading hotel, the McLure House, to work as a bellboy. By the time he was sixteen he had taught himself to handle the hotel's books and at nineteen he was the untitled manager. The photograph to the left shows Mr. Statler when he was about twelve; the one on this page shows him as a young entrepreneur.

To celebrate E. M. Statler's fiftieth birthday in 1913, his family gathered at his Buffalo mansion on Soldier's Place.

The family photograph, shown above, was taken to commemorate the occasion. Mr. Statler is seated in the second row center, holding one of his two adopted children (later he adopted two more). To his right is his first wife, the former Mary Manderbach, holding his other child, and to his left is his mother, then in her eighties. Also shown are his brothers and sisters with their husbands, wives, and children, who could not be accurately identified.

Mr. Statler already numbered among his hotel properties the first Buffalo Statler and also the Cleveland, Detroit, and St. Louis Statler hotels, and was a millionaire.

great prosperity came to the town and their hotel was continually full.

Show people, drummers, farmers, merchants, river boat gamblers, they all stopped at the McLure. The guests included William Gillette, touring in the play *Sherlock Holmes;* Mrs. Fiske, Maurice Barrymore; the Dockstader Minstrels; Sarah Bernhardt; William Wrigley selling soap before he thought of chewing gum; John D. Rockefeller traveling to and from his newly discovered oil fields.

When the workmen in the LaBelle glassworks crossed the river on Saturday nights they were not headed for the McLure House, to be sure. Their earthy pleasures were to be found in the dark streets near the riverfront, and their adventures supplied topics for boastful talk back at the glass factory during the following week. Nor were the young glory hole boys protected from the lurid details; they formed a rapt audience.

The Statler brothers made their first trip to Wheeling about a month after starting work in the factory. Along with a couple of other glory hole friends they began exploring the city and it was a time before Charlie noticed that Ellsworth had disappeared. This fact held little interest for the rest of the boys but Charlie felt the responsibility of his years and began a search for his brother. He found him standing across the street from the McLure House.

"What happened to you?" he demanded angrily.

"Nothin'."

"Where'd you go to?"

"I come here."

"I can see that, but whatcha doin' here?"

"Just watchin'."

"Watchin' that? — The hotel? Ya can't watch a building, it doesn't do nothin'."

Ellsworth shrugged his shoulders. He had given an honest explanation of his action and if his brother couldn't understand, that was his problem. Charlie was sufficiently concerned to report it to their mother when they returned home that night. She didn't take the matter up with Ellsworth until the next day when the other children were out of the house. She did not reproach him, she merely asked him for an explanation.

Taking a big breath, he told her all about it in a rush of words. He told of the shining carriages that pulled up in front of the hotel; of the beautiful women who had feathers and ribbons all over their hats; of the uniformed man who stood in front of the hotel and did nothing but open the door for the gentlemen and ladies to enter; of the sounds of laughter that spilled out of the building from time to time. He concluded with the words, "That must be the most beautiful building in the world."

Mary was caught up with her son's vision and she signed wistfully. The father, who had heard it all from his chair on the other side of the room, said heavily, "Sodom and Gomorrah."

She turned on him impatiently. "That's not a very nice thing to say, William. I'm certain there are many fine God-fearing people who go into a hotel."

He shook his head. "The trail of the serpent is over them all."

William could always find Scripture to support his point of view, thereby placing his opponent in the untenable position of arguing against God's word. Mary knew his method and she met it the only way she could — by silence. Moreover, the next day brought the family a tragedy that pushed the hotel question far into the background; it was death.

The Statler children frequently swam in the Ohio River. The water was torpid and shallow near the shore, there was no hint of danger, yet on this afternoon John (a year older than Ellsworth) was seized with a cramp, slipped beneath the water and drowned. Charles and Ellsworth were nearby and they dived time and again but the muddy waters hid John until it was too late. When they finally found him and pulled him ashore he was quite dead.

The panoply of death is not for the poor. There was a hearse for hire in the local livery stable; it had beveled plate glass windows that framed drapes of pleated black silk fringed with silver balls. At each corner there rose a sculptured pillar topped with a large black bow. Matching black horses pulled this apparition, this thing of sombre show, this public ritual of sorrow.

Such "honoring of the dead" was not for the Statlers. William placed his son in a pine box of his own making, nailed down the lid and placed it in a flat bed wagon drawn by a spavined horse.

William had warned his wife there would be no eulogy. "God will judge our boy with justice and mercy," he said. "Ain't fittin' for us tryin' to give Him a sales talk."

At the graveside William intoned, "The Lord gave, and the Lord hath taken away. Blessed be the name of the Lord."

"Amen," murmured the family.

"Whether we live, we live unto the Lord; and whether we die, we die unto the Lord; whether we live therefore, or die, we are the Lord's."

"Amen."

"God shall wipe away all tears from their eyes; and there shall be no more death, neither sorrow, nor crying, neither shall there be any more pain: for the former things are passed away."

As the family listened they found comfort in the ancient words.

Mourning the dead had to be brief in the Statler family; the pressures of living made it so. The week following the burial, Ellsworth said to his mother, "Ma, do you know how much money the bellboys at the McLure House get?"

"I don't want to talk about it now," she said.

"Six dollars a month!" he said. "Also, their meals and the tips from the drummers. Sometimes the tips are one dollar in a single day!"

"What are the tips for?" she asked, curiosity winning.

"For carrying satchels and sample cases and running errands and things."

"But isn't that what the six dollars pay is for?"

"Sure, but you get tips anyway."

"Don't seem right and proper. If a person is paid to do a job he should do it without expecting to be . . . well, bribed!"

"That's not the way it is at all, Ma."

"That's the way it appears to me," she said firmly, dismissing the subject.

The boy persisted. "I could refuse the tips," he said.

She reached out and pulled him against her, kissing the top of his head. "No, darling, you're too young to work in that place. Maybe Charles . . . but not you. Not yet."

"When, Ma? When can I work there?"

"Oh, not until you're in your teens," she replied, trying to make the date as vague as possible.

For the boy it was specific. Immediately after his thirteenth birthday he appeared in the lobby of the McLure House and began his campaign for a job.

CHAPTER 6

LIFE OF A BELLBOY

The desk clerk tried a number of techniques to get rid of the boy who appeared before him each night: silence and then sarcasm, Olympian ignoring followed by stern dismissal, finally even friendly advice to stop wasting his time. None of these worked; the boy had a stubborn patience.

At last the clerk said, "If you're gonna hang around here you might as well do some work. One of the bellboys is sick and you can take his place for tonight. *Just for tonight!*"

"Yes, sir," Ellsworth grinned. There was no question in his mind but that he could make the job permanent.

The bellboy job was easier than stoking a glory hole, but not a whole lot. The McLure House was five stories tall, and though an elevator was eventually installed, it was for the use of the guests and the manager, not for the bellboys. The guests on the top floors always seemed to demand more service than those on the lower ones. By use of a button in his room a guest could summon room service, but not indicate what kind of service he required; the bellboy had to climb the stairs to learn this. If it was ice water, the boy had to return to the kitchen on the main floor, chip some ice into a pitcher and then climb back up again to deliver it. If the guest wanted heat, the boy climbed down to the basement to get a scuttle of coal and an armload of kindling, then climb back to the room to lay and ignite the fire. If he was not skillful, he might have to return several times to reignite it.

Not infrequently a bellboy was summoned by a nervous guest to "sniff the hall." Kerosene lamps had recently given way to the more modern illumination provided by gas, and guests would sometimes blow out the flame upon retiring and forget entirely to turn off the flow of gas. If a guest wanted a bath there was a public bathroom down the hall and a bellboy would supply hot water and receive the extra charge made for such facility.

Ellsworth found himself on a constant dog-trot during those first days. Not only was he out to make the job permanent, but he had a consuming curiosity about every aspect of the hotel business. The very first thing that surprised him was the bleakness of the guest rooms. He had assumed that the grandeur of the lobby and the public rooms would be duplicated in the bedrooms, and was disappointed to find this was not so.

The McLure House was better in this respect than most hotels, but none of them felt any particular concern about the nighttime comfort of the traveler. When a man was in his room he was not spending money in the bar or the billiard parlor or at the cigar counter, or in any of the diversions offered in the rest of the city. It was wasted time, as far as the hotel management was concerned, and it seemed poor business indeed to make the bedroom so attractive a man would want to stay in it any longer than to sleep.

The mattresses were invariably lumpy and sagged in the middle. The sheets were coarse and scratchy and the comforters heavy without being warm. The bedsteads were either of rusting iron or of oak gummed over with thick layers of peeling varnish. The plumbing consisted of a pitcher of water, a large bowl, a slop jar and a spittoon. The gas fixture was located so that it failed to illuminate either the cracked mirror above the washbowl, or a book if held while in bed. On the back of the door was a large hook to accommodate overcoat, coat, vest, pants, shirt, or whatever else was to be hung up. There was one straight chair that could be used in place of hangers — two chairs if a double room.

The disadvantage of the double bed was that if business was brisk the weary traveler might find a bedmate assigned to him. And always of the same sex!

"Boat day" was the big event of the week for the McLure House. The river packets approaching from the north floated down the Ohio from Pittsburgh; those from the south steamed up the river from Cincinnati. The major boats were named *Keystone State, Queen City, Kanawha,* and the *Virginian* — each described by its owner as "a floating palace of unparalleled luxury." Actually, they were all pretty much the same. They were large flat boats with shallow draft and superstructure of three decks. The lower deck was open for easy handling of freight and livestock; the second deck contained the private cabins and the public rooms where the river gamblers plied their trade; the third, or "Texas" deck, had quarters for officers and crew. They were propelled by great paddle wheels set at the side or at the stern.

Two years before Ellsworth became a bellboy, Mark Twain had written of his own childhood love affair with these boats. In *Life on the Mississippi* he wrote: "(Their smokestacks were) a spraying crown of plumes ... gilt deer horns over the big bell; gaudy symbolic pictures on the paddle box ... porcelain knob and oil picture on every stateroom door ... big chandeliers every little way, each an April shower of glittering glass drops ... in the ladies' cabin a pink and white Wilton carpet, as soft as mush."

The river boat announced its arrival with a full-throated cry from its whistle and much of the town ran down to the wharf to watch its stately approach. A cargo boom swung the gangplank up off the forward deck and laid it from ship to dock. The lobby of the McLure House was soon full of drummers checking in, and all the bellboys ran about with luggage, ice water, hot water, coal and kindling. There was a brief lull in the lobby after the drummers had gone upstairs, but soon they were back down again and headed for the bar.

It was a warm and welcoming room with a free lunch counter that held pickled pigs feet, a variety of cold meats, a stack of rye bread and a bowl of hard-boiled eggs. Hung above the bar and dominating the room was a painting of a life-sized nude — a lady with a shy smile and heroic proportions.

Presiding over the bar with humor but firmness was Tom Duffy. He was a good listener, as all good bartenders should be, and became the confidant of many a lonely drummer. He could also be a good talker on occasion, and since he had traveled extensively he had a variety of exotic stories with which to enliven a long evening.

One of Duffy's greatest admirers was the new bellboy, Ellsworth. There was mutual admiration here for Duffy saw the seriousness and the ambition in the boy and while he had no ambition for himself, he admired it in others — especially in the young.

"Mr. Duffy, you speak good English, don't you?" Ellsworth asked him one day.

"I do," the bartender said.

"I didn't have much schooling," the boy said.

"So I hear," Duffy smiled. "And you'd like me to correct you when you make an error."

"Yes, sir, I've got a lot to learn about this business and it's important that I talk right. When I seen how well you talk . . ."

Duffy raised his hand. "Never say 'I seen', always say 'I saw.' That's the proper way."

"When I *saw* how well you spoke . . ."

"Don't you mean that you *heard* me speak?"

The boy thought for a moment. "Sure, that's what I meant. Gee, you have to think about it, don't you?"

"Not after you have the proper habits, then it comes without your thinking about it."

"Will you help me, Mr. Duffy?"

"I sure will, kid. We'll have a lesson every afternoon about this time, when business is slow."

And they did.

The McLures were accustomed to having bellboys who were lazy, or stupid, or insolent, or a combination of all three, and when they suddenly had one who was serious and quick and hard-working they were at first disbelieving. But when the first year had passed with no let-up in Ellsworth's enthusiasm for his job, they were simply mystified. It did not occur to them that an uneducated boy of fourteen could be ambitious. This quality, it seemed to them, was something that came (or didn't come) with manhood; a boy should be concerned with swimming and fishing and playing ball. They could not know that this slight, sober-faced boy found hotel work the greatest fun.

In the summer of 1878 the Reverend William Statler died. It seemed likely that he had wanted to die; certainly he had been unsuited to this world. The family buried him next to his son John, and on the trip back from the cemetery Mary Statler clung to the arm of, not her oldest child, but the next to youngest — Ellsworth. Without anyone putting it into words, they all knew that this fifteen-year-old boy was now the head of the family.

That evening when he went to work he walked up to Bernie McLure and said, "Mr. McLure, I think it's time you made me head bellboy."

The man pulled at his chin a moment and then said, "Ellsworth, I guess you're right."

From that day on the bell line doubled its efficiency. Ellsworth knew all the dodges to avoid work and tolerated none of them in the boys under him. In retaliation, they nicknamed him "Colonel." The resentment was understandable, many of them were older, most had been there longer, and some had considerably more education. Despite all this, the resentment was short-lived and the nickname became one of respect, almost affection.

Ellsworth never gave an order to the boys merely for the sake of showing off his authority; he only asked them to do things they knew they should do. They finally realized that Ellsworth had a drive for success that none of them shared, or even wanted to share, and so there was no jealousy.

"Oh, he'll be a big shot one day," they said to each other, "but he's sure gonna miss a lot of fun in life."

As head bellboy, Ellsworth decided he had enough stature to approach the various department heads and question them about their work. He wanted to know how every part of the hotel functioned, from housekeeper right down to engineer. He was impossible to brush off and he doggedly kept questioning until he understood.

One day Harry McLure said to him, "Ellsworth, you're a good boy but sometimes you get people all upset. You argue with them all the time. Why do you do that?"

"I'm not arguing, Mr. McLure, I'm just asking questions."

"But you never seem satisfied with the answers. You keep hectoring."

"I don't mean to, but I gotta keep asking until I understand, don't I?"

"Until you understand what, boy?"

"How to run a hotel. Someday I'm going to run the biggest hotel in the world ... and I got a lot to learn."

In future years, whenever Harry McLure told this story, he'd say, "I'll tell you something funny. When that fifteen-year-old kid with about a third-grade education said that to me, damned if I didn't believe him. Don't ask me to explain why, I just did. Whenever Ellsworth Statler said he was going to do something, by God, he did it."

CHAPTER 7

HOTEL McLURE

Shortly after becoming head bellboy, Ellsworth began carrying a small notebook into which he entered ideas for self-improvement. At first the notes concerned rules of grammar, but soon they broadened to include his observations about hotel management.

One day an irate guest came marching out of the dining room and up to the desk clerk. "That waiter in there is disputing me," he stormed. "I want you to decide who is right."

"About what?" the clerk asked.

"About our dispute, that's what. It doesn't make any difference *what* we're disputing, I want you to say who is right."

"Without hearing his side of the story?"

"Without hearing either side of the story."

The clerk suspected that the man was slightly drunk. He shrugged his shoulders and said, "Well, since I've known the waiter longer than I've known you, I'll have to say he was right."

The man went immediately to his room, packed his suitcase and checked out of the hotel. The head bellboy, who had observed this, made an entry in his notebook.

Frank McLure sauntered up to him and said, "Well, Ellsworth, what did you put in your little black book this time?"

The bellboy held up his notebook for his employer

to read. A single sentence was scrawled across a page: "The guest is *always* right."

"Well now, Ellsworth," McLure said patronizingly, "aren't you being a little hard on the waiter, not even hearing his side of the story?"

"No, sir. My theory is that he shouldn't argue with a guest, no matter what."

"Hmmmm. It's a nice theory, but . . ."

"We lost a customer, didn't we?"

McLure had no response to that, and he walked away deep in thought. A month later Ellsworth Statler was promoted to night desk clerk.

The night clerk was, for all practical purposes, night manager. He not only had to oversee the working of the various departments, but he had guests who were occasionally amorous, not infrequently drunk, and sometimes just plain cantankerous. If a late poker game was being played in one of the rooms and was disturbing the neighbors, it was the clerk's job to quiet the game without offending the players. If a guest came off the street with an accommodating lady obviously not his wife, the clerk had to inform her that she could not do her accommodating in the McLure, and he had to tell her this without appearing a prude or acting the least bit censorious. If a guest became drunk and disorderly, the night clerk had to remove him from the public rooms and guide him to bed with a firm but comradely hand.

It was a job that required patience and judgment and tolerance — qualities that come to a man with years, if at all. The amazement was, not that young Statler did his job so well, but that he did it at all. He could only be described as a premature adult.

One night a guest returned to the hotel about midnight and he was drunk to the point of falling down. Ellsworth directed a bellboy to escort him safely to bed. The bellboy returned five minutes later and started across the lobby toward the bar.

"Did he order something?" Ellsworth called to the boy.

"Yeah. A bottle of champagne."

"Take him a bottle of carbonated water instead. He won't know the difference."

"Okay," the bellboy replied, giving Ellsworth a conspiratorial wink.

Ellsworth was not setting up a nice little racket, as the boy thought, for he meticulously entered into the man's account the price of one bottle of carbonated water. The next day the guest looked up the night clerk to shake his hand.

"Son, I want to thank you," he said. "You not only saved me some money but you saved me from even a worse hangover than I have."

When Ellsworth was sixteen the McLures retired from active management of their hotel and Fred and E. J. Norton began to run things. These brothers were pleasant, easygoing men who enjoyed the convivial life of a hotel and saw no reason to work very hard.

Of all the hotel chores, the one hated most by Fred Norton was keeping the books. He would allow entries to pile up, postpone paying bills, and rarely had a guest's account up-to-date when the man wished to check out.

One evening a guest missed a boat connection because he had to wait twenty minutes for his bill. He stalked out of the lobby with loud denunciations of the hotel and a promise never to return. That evening the young night clerk made a suggestion to his boss.

"I have a lot of spare time at night," he said, "and if you'd teach me bookkeeping I could keep the books up-to-date."

"You mean it, Ellsworth?" the delighted man exclaimed. "You'll take over the books?"

"If you'll teach me. I can learn fast."

"Son, you've got a deal."

By the end of the week Ellsworth had assumed complete responsibility for the books and Fred Norton gave a sigh of relief. It was a premature sigh of relief. Ellsworth Statler discovered that the books constituted a fever chart, revealed the health or illness of all the various departments in the hotel, and he began to bombard Fred Norton with suggestions for improved efficiency.

"I think our room rates need some revision, Mr. Norton," he announced one evening. Fred Norton gave a heavy sigh, but that did not discourage the boy. "We have two-dollar rooms and three-dollar rooms. If a man and wife take a three-dollar room at double rates, they pay six dollars. But if they take a two-dollar and a three-dollar room they pay a total of only five dollars and yet occupy two rooms, making us lose the income of that second room."

"Damn it, Statler," Norton exploded, "you just keep the books and we'll run the hotel."

The following week the night clerk raised another point. "Mr. Norton, the food in the dining room isn't very good."

"Oh?" Norton said. And then with heavy sarcasm, "Did you find that fact in the books?"

"No, sir, from eating in the dining room."

"The food seems all right to me."

"You don't eat what is served the guests. You eat in your room and the chef cooks different food for you. I think it would be a good idea for you to eat in the dining room."

"Lordy, lordy," Norton intoned, rolling his eyes heavenward, "now he wants to run my private life."

"I've been reading about how the dining room is run on big trans-Atlantic luxury liners," the boy continued implacably. "The Captain eats with the passengers, even invites some of the important ones to dine at his table. It might be a good idea for us to establish the Manager's Table and invite our more important guests to eat there with you."

Norton walked away without even replying.

Ellsworth had been night clerk for two years when the Norton brothers announced that the McLure House would be closed for extensive remodeling. Ellsworth Statler would be out of a job for at least six months, and maybe longer if the Nortons didn't rehire him when the place reopened. Certainly he had been the burr under their saddle, and this might be a chance for them to eliminate the pain.

Both Ellsworth and Charlie (who had remained a bellboy) went to work for an uncle who made buggies in Bridgeport. The pay was poor and after a few weeks the boys took jobs in a Wheeling steel mill.

Work in the mill was no more difficult than it had been in the glassworks, but Ellsworth had changed. The hotel business had hooked him and he knew that somehow, somewhere he had to get back into it. Drummers had spread stories about the young man's efficiency and soon he received an offer of a job as day clerk in the Butchtel Hotel in Akron, Ohio. He accepted at once.

When the McLure House reopened the following summer the Nortons, apparently deciding that a burr was good for them, asked Ellsworth to return as day clerk. He wanted very much to return but he posed a condition; he wanted to lease the billiard room that opened off the lobby. From his work on the McLure books he knew that the room could be a good source of revenue, but also that it had been slowly going to pot. More and more Wheeling's working class drifters filled the place with coarse talk. The drummers and the town's better class began to stay away and the Nortons had been undecided whether to reopen the room at all. They were happy to place the problem in young Statler's hands.

The first thing Ellsworth did upon returning to the McLure House was to inspect his newly leased property, the billiard room. It was a discouraging sight; the floor was stained with tobacco juice that had been poorly aimed toward the spittoons, the table cushions were burned from untended cigars, the felt ripped and patched, the cues were warped and many were missing their tips, and the balls were nicked and scarred. It was obvious that the room would have to be completely refurnished and filled with new equipment before he could expect to win back the drummers and the better citizens of Wheeling. There was one small problem — he had no money.

At this point young Statler learned a fact of business life: Hard cash is not the only currency in business, there is also something called credit.

One of the drummers whom Ellsworth had met and served in the hotel was George Meyers, a sales agent for Brunswick Balke-Colender Company, manufacturers of billiard equipment. He checked into the McLure House a a week after the reopening and stuck out his hand to the day clerk.

"Ellsworth," he said, "I'm sure glad to see you back."

"Thank you, Mr. Meyers."

"When you're on the desk I always know I'm going to get good service," He signed the register, then glanced back over his shoulder toward the billiard room from which loud bursts of profanity occasionally came. He said, "I heard that you took a lease on that room."

"Yes, sir."

"Do you know what that room needs?"

"A better class of player."

"You're right, there. But before you can attract the business and professional men ..."

"I need all new equipment," Statler interrupted.

"You've been thinking this through, I see."

"Yes, sir. With new equipment in there I could raise the prices and freeze out the bums. But . . ."

"You don't have the money right now."

"That's about it," Statler said ruefully. "But I'll get it . . . one day."

"I'm sure you will, but let's not wait. I think I can persuade my company to let you have the new tables on credit."

Statler looked at him, disbelieving. "Without any security or . . . or, what do you call it, collateral?"

"Oh, we'd want collateral. Your word!" He grinned at Statler and said, "Son, I get around this country a good deal but I've never seen a young man who is more square and hardworking than you. And I'm not giving you something for nothing. It's good business for my company to have decently run billiard rooms. Billiards is a game for gentlemen and you can help us keep it that way. Do we have a deal?"

"Yes, sir!" Statler grinned.

CHAPTER 8

YOUTHFUL ENTREPRENEUR

Mary Statler shook her head and said, "No, Ellsworth, no, no, no!"

"Ma, listen to me a minute," he said. "Don't go saying no until you've heard."

She sighed and clamped her mouth shut in a thin line of resistance. She would listen but her mouth warned him that she would not change her mind.

"It's the most modern billiard room in the whole state. I had oak paneling put halfway up the side of the walls. There are real leather chairs for spectators or for the use of the players between games. All the tables are brand new, and above each one is a solid brass chandelier, and I have them polished every week until they look like gold. It's a beautiful room, Ma."

"It's a billiard room," she countered.

"Some of the most important men in town come to my room."

She sniffed. "If they have nothing better to do than poke balls with a stick..." She didn't bother to finish the sentence.

Referring to his youngest brother Osceola, Ellsworth said, "All that O.C. would have to do is rack up the balls for the players, keep the cue tips in repair and keep the place swept up. He'd make a lot of money in tips."

"He's too young."

"I'm not suggesting he stop school, just come in for a few hours after school."

"He's too young to be around those hotel people."

"Ma, he's no younger than I was when I went to work."

She reached over to touch his hand. "You were always different." Her eyes softened with memory. "I think I always knew you were different, from the day you were born back in Gettysburg. Such a sober child. I never had to worry about you. Pa always thought you might get the call, become a preacher. Perhaps, if we'd been able to give you the proper education..."

"No, Ma," he said gently. "I never wanted to be a preacher. I want to do what I'm doing right now, I'm going to make money, Ma, and buy you a house of your own and..."

She shook her head, tears in her eyes. "I depend on you like you was a full man. It don't seem right that a boy should have such a burden. You should be having fun instead of working so hard."

"Work can be fun," he said.

She had never found it so, nor had her husband. But this boy lived in a different world. Perhaps it was a better world, she didn't know, but she mistrusted it.

"When O.C. is at work I'll be there, Ma. I'll see that nothing happens to him."

"He's so young," she sighed.

Ellsworth placed his younger brother in the billiard room to further raise the tone of the place. What he did not anticipate was that O.C. was to make the room famous. During his spare time and when a table was available, O.C. practiced the game and soon became expert. There were many drummers who had high opinions of their own game, and when they walked into the room and saw a boy in knee pants and long, black, ribbed stockings make a few creditable shots, they rather patronizingly challenged him to a game. More often than not, they lost.

O.C.'s fame spread and drummers often went miles out

of their way to stay overnight at the McLure House and play the kid. Ellsworth invited professionals to come to Wheeling and give exhibitions of their skill and play the boy. On such occasions many of the local citizens crowded in to watch and cheer the hometown boy. As a result, the room became a whopping financial success.

After he had paid off his indebtedness to the Brunswick Balke-Colender Company, Ellsworth had a talk with O.C. "You're as much responsible for the success of the room as I am," he said. "And I'm going to make you a partner. From now on you'll get half of the profits."

"Gosh, Ell, thanks," the boy said.

"Just one thing," Ellsworth continued, "some of our guests like to place bets on a game. We can't stop that but we can make sure that we're not involved. When you're in a game with somebody, I don't care who, you've got to do your level best. If I ever hear of you throwing a game, you're no longer a partner. You won't even be working for me. You're out! Got that straight?"

"Sure, I understand. Don't you worry about me."

"I'm not worrying about you, but Ma. I don't want any of us to ever do anything to bring shame on her."

O.C. nodded soberly. The partnership in the billiard room was to bring him $2,500 a year, and he was not going to do anything to jeopardize that bonanza.

Watching the crowds come and go in the billiard room, a friend remarked to Fred Norton that his young clerk was making a pretty good thing out of a room that had almost shut down. Norton rubbed his chin ruefully and said, "Ellsworth does seem to have an instinct for undeveloped opportunities."

That turned out to be the understatement of Fred Norton's life.

The McLure House gave railway men special rates, thirty-five cents for a bed and thirty-five cents for a meal, and as a result the hotel became their headquarters. They could be seen each day lined up against the long bar, watch in one hand and dice in the other, gambling for drinks until it was time to run for their trains.

The young desk clerk questioned them about their work, just as he did all guests, and received information he could put to use. The railroads would offer mileage tickets in 1,000-mile units for two cents a mile. The purchaser could resell them in short mileage units for two and a half cents a mile, which was still cheaper than they could be purchased at the station.

"Mr. Norton," Statler said to his boss one evening, "I've got an idea."

"I dare say you have," the man grinned.

"It's a new service for our guests. As things are now they have to walk all the way to the station to buy their railroad tickets, usually hours before traintime, and it's very inconvenient. I'd like to put up a ticket office here in the lobby, right next to the entrance to the billiard room. I think they'd appreciate the service and we could make a profit."

"Well, I suppose we can try it," Norton said dubiously.

Statler designed the booth and when it was completed it attracted the eye of every man and woman who entered the lobby. Its wainscot matched that in the billiard room, and above the counter was a dramatic canopy made of cherrywood jointed and steam-glued together in the most intricate design. Train travel seemed twice as exciting when the ticket was purchased at such a glamorous place. From the opening day business was brisk, and the service added luster to the reputation of the McLure House. This was the first transportation department ever to function in an American hotel.

The ancient and honored game of billiards (played in England during Shakespeare's time) began to have competition from a game called bowling. This game was first introduced to the New World around 1650 by the Dutch who called it nine pins and played it outdoors. The first indoor game was played on wooden alleys in New York in 1840 and slowly its popularity moved across the country until it entered Wheeling in the early 1890's. Young Statler watched its approach with some concern, for he had a vested interest in billiards. Would this new craze empty his billiard room? He decided not to fight bowling but to join it if the opportunity presented itself. It did.

A number of prominent Wheeling citizens banded together to form a private bowling club. By buying stock at $10 a share they raised $1,500 with which they leased the Musee, an old vaudeville house, and installed alleys. The venture was a success in that the members did not have to rub elbows with the ordinary people, but the club was soon in financial trouble. The income just didn't meet the expenses, and none of the members wanted to increase the dues.

At this point young Statler appeared and offered to buy 51 % of the stock at $9 a share. The offer was accepted; Statler bought the stock and dissolved the club. Going once more into debt, he added four alleys to the four that existed, installed eight billiard tables, constructed a cigar counter, partitioned off a barber shop, and hired his brother William as manager.

When the "New Musee" opened it became a great success, not only because the equipment was good and the atmosphere genteel, but because young Statler had a sure touch in promotion. He helped organize various leagues and sponsored tournaments with a $500 prize. This was not an original idea with him, but he adopted it and carried it out with more energy, more imagination.

Pleased with the success but not satisfied, Statler brooded over the fact that there was a large section of the Musee that was vacant. Years in the future when he had become a legend in the hotel business, there sprang up among hotel men the phrase "to Statlerize." This meant to get action and income from every possible square foot of lobby space. The New Musee was about to be Statlerized.

One evening at home he was eating a pie made by his sister Alabama. "Bama," he said, "you make the best pie in town." And there it was, the idea he had been waiting for. He struck the table with his hand and cried out, "Bama, you want to go into business with me? We'll open a pie shop in the Musee. We'll serve your homemade pies and the best coffee available."

They did just that, and the Musee's "Pie Shop" became the most popular snack bar in town.

Statler's four enterprises gave him the substantial income of $10,000 a year. He bought his mother a new home on Wheeling Island, and he numbered among his friends the town's outstanding businessmen. It was widely predicted that Ellsworth Milton Statler had a great future in Wheeling. But his destiny was grander than that — and more tragic.

CHAPTER 9

ELLICOTT SQUARE RESTAURANT

Young Statler was popular with the business leaders of Wheeling because he was both successful and "a man's man." He enjoyed fishing and drinking and playing poker — but all in moderation — all as a background for the almost constant dialogue about business.

This acceptance by men of substance could be a heady thing for any young man, and especially for one who started work at nine years of age in a glass factory, but on the whole he handled his success modestly. He listened more than he spoke; when he spoke it was to the point. Mostly he was grave but he laughed easily at the new humor in the land — scatological jokes about traveling salesmen.

He continued to carry the little notebook into which he entered pointers for self-improvement. He found his philosophy of life in the words of the Scottish poet, Alexander Smith, and copied them into his notebook: ". . . failure and success are not accidents as we so frequently suppose, but the strictest justice. If you do your fair day's work, you are certain to get your fair day's wage — in praise or pudding, whichever happens to suit your taste."

In the spring of 1894 Statler and several friends went to Canada to fish. They returned by way of Buffalo, New York, where he came upon the block-long Ellicott Square Building, then under construction. There was a sign which announced that upon completion this would be "The Biggest Office Building in the World."

The bigness of the building drew him powerfully. Some men cannot resist ships sailing for distant lands, some cannot resist alcohol, some a beautiful woman; Statler's weakness was a big building, and after some thought he devised a plan for becoming a part of this imposing project.

John N. Scatcherd was president of the Ellicott Square Company and he received the young man from Wheeling and listened to him with kindly skepticism. Statler bubbled over with plans for putting a restaurant on the ground floor of the building.

Finally Scatcherd broke in. "Son, have you had any experience in the restaurant business?"

"Yes, sir. In Wheeling . . ."

"No, I mean have you had any experience in the restaurant business in *Buffalo?*"

"Well, no, sir."

"Buffalo has a reputation as a poor restaurant town. I don't know why it is, but the folks here just aren't in the habit of eating out."

Statler grinned. "We'll have to change their habits."

"I just want to be fair with you, let you know what you're facing. The annual rent of that first floor area is eight thousand five hundred dollars."

"Will you give me a verbal option on the area for one month while I raise the money?"

"You have it."

They shook hands on it, and Statler rushed back to Wheeling.

When he approached his friends and associates for backing he was brimming with enthusiasm and confidence and acted as if he was doing them a favor. It could well have been pointed out to him that the success of a small pie shop in Wheeling did not really fit him for operating an enormous restaurant in Buffalo with an annual rental of $8,500, but no one did so. The town accepted Statler's measurement of himself, sometimes even going beyond. He was the golden boy who could not fail at anything. A Statler mystique was in the process of creation.

George House, who owned a large and successful credit store, unhesitatingly underwrote the $8,500 rental; George Meyers again prevailed upon the Brunswick Balke-Colender Company to supply, on credit, $17,000 worth of restaurant equipment; the John Van Range Company, makers of kitchenware, accepted Statler's unsecured personal note for $11,000. To this pool of credit and cash Statler added his own savings of $10,000 and headed back for Buffalo.

On the way there he stopped off in Akron, Ohio, to secure a wife. He married Mary Manderbach, a woman he had met while working there as a desk clerk in the Butchtel Hotel. This marriage revealed a good deal about Statler, for she was not the type of woman one would normally expect a fiercely ambitious man to marry. She was a square and plain woman with little more education than Statler had, and with no flair for either clothes or conversation. If a man had either social or political ambitions she would be of little assistance. But if a man wanted comfort and security at home, if he wanted simplicity, if he wanted a sounding board for his ideas, if he wanted an undemanding woman of infinite patience and blind loyalty, Mary Manderbach was the right choice.

Upon arrival in Buffalo, Statler installed his bride in an apartment and turned to devote approximately eighteen hours out of each day to his restaurant. If the bride was lonesome it was well that she become accustomed to the condition, for this pattern of living was to change very little over the coming years.

Despite his limited experience in restaurant management, Statler came up with many innovations. He devised a new kind of service table to increase the waitress's efficiency. It rolled on wheels and contained several compartments for cutlery, linens, glasses, butter chips and condiments. This saved the waitress long trips to a sideboard, or even kitchen, for supplies each time she made up a table. To seat the maximum number of diners with the greatest privacy he designed octagon-shaped dining tables. These were simple innovations but most effective in speeding a rapid flow of customers.

On July 4, 1895, Statler's Ellicott Square Restaurant opened. All over town patriotic speeches were being made, firecrackers were exploding and flags were waving, but very few citizens entered the new restaurant to eat. Nor did the number increase significantly the following day, nor in the days and weeks to come. He had figured everything out mathematically; he could accommodate 500 diners at a sitting, and with such mass production of meals he could operate on a small margin of profit per meal. What his careful calculations did not provide for was the absence of the 500 diners. John Scatcherd had warned him about the eating habits of this town but Statler ignored the older man's words with youthful confidence.

By the end of the summer his cash reserve had run out and his creditors were restless. The local wholesale grocers demanded to be paid within five days. Statler went to William H. Love, a leading Buffalo attorney, and said, "They're trying to push me into Lake Erie. I wish you'd look into my affairs and advise me."

Love looked and figured and reported, "The best thing you can do is go into bankruptcy."

"Hell's fire, no!" Statler exploded. "I didn't come to Buffalo to be a bankrupt."

"If you did, you could pay your creditors off at about ten cents on a dollar, and they'd have to accept it."

"I intend to pay my creditors one hundred cents on a dollar. What I want from you is advice on how to stall them off until I can get reorganized."

"That may not be easy," the lawyer said.

It wasn't easy. The grocer, smallest creditor of them all with a bill of $180, marched into the restaurant with a court order and a sheriff. Statler had $180 in the cash register and paid it over. He was free of the grocer but now the other small creditors began to panic and they all ran to court. Also, they were threatening to attach his other assets, the billiard room and the Musee and the Pie Shop back in Wheeling. It looked like everything was about to go down the drain. The golden boy was fast tarnishing.

Statler discussed it with his wife, or rather he narrated the problem to her. To go into bankruptcy would take from his shoulders an enormous burden of debt, but would it be fair to his creditors? Or was it just stubborn pride that was preventing him from doing what seemed to be essential?

On the other hand, suppose he was able to stall his creditors, suppose he got a year's extension, what then? What could be done to make the restaurant a success the second year that had not been done the first year? All the logic seemed to point to voluntary bankruptcy, unloading his debts and making a new start in some other town. It was not uncommon practice in the business world, so why shouldn't he do it?

At last he stopped talking, slumped in a chair and stared grimly at his feet. His wife said gently, "I know you'll do what is right, Ellsworth."

What was right? When did a man quit? When did he hang on? When did he surrender? When fight?

He stood up abruptly and went into the bedroom and began to undress. As he took off his jacket a small black book fell out of the pocket. It was the book in which he had entered all the self-improvement bits of philosophy. He picked it up and leafed through the pages, a smile of irony on his face. He had neglected to enter anything that applied to operating a 500-chair restaurant in Buffalo, New York.

Or had he? He found scribbled across one page a quotation from a man named Ovid. He had never gotten around to look up who Ovid was. He couldn't even remember how or where he had seen the words printed . . . some magazine, he thought. The words were: "Either do not attempt at all, or go through with it."

They were commonplace enough words, and yet they carried an impact. Statler read them again, slowly, aloud: "Either do not attempt at all, or go through with it."

He picked up the phone beside the bed and put through a call to his lawyer. "Mr. Love, I've reached a decision. No bankruptcy! I'm gonna fight it out! I want you to call a meeting of all my creditors so I can talk to them face to face."

A half dozen men gathered in Love's office. They were the creditors and they were hostile and suspicious. They reasoned that if Statler was ready to pay them what he owed, he would not have called this meeting. Therefore, this could be only an attempt to bamboozle them. Well, just let him try!

After a few minutes of heavy silence Statler strode into the room, nodded his head in a general greeting and took a seat beside his lawyer.

Love opened the meeting with the announcement that he had a few telegrams he wished to read. Just at that moment John Scatcherd, president of the Ellicott Square Company, walked into the office, apologized for his tardiness and said that the press of another meeting would not allow him to stay.

"I could not pass up this opportunity to say a few words to you men," Scatcherd said to the other creditors. "I want you to know that I have the greatest confidence in Mr. Statler. He is attempting something unique in our town, getting the public into the habit of eating out. If he succeeds it will benefit all of us. I think he will succeed if we give him enough time to work out his problems. I, for one, intend to give him that time. Statler is good for Buffalo, and I hope we will be good for him."

Thereupon Scatcherd thanked them and left the office. Statler watched the faces of the men opposite him and he saw bitter little smiles. These men were not unaware that Scatcherd had his rent guaranteed by George House in Wheeling.

"I have some telegrams here," Love said again, "and since they are from the major creditors I'm sure you'll be interested in them."

From George House came, "I have the utmost confidence in Ellsworth Statler and will stand by him."

George Meyers, speaking in behalf of Brunswick Balke-Colender, wired: "Sure Statler will make a success of his restaurant. His credit remains Grade A with us."

The men in the room seemed unimpressed; they considered Meyers and House part of "the Wheeling crowd" to which Statler belonged. No telling what they might be up to; might even be secretly siphoning off the assets to themselves.

There were other pledges of support. One came from Taylor & Taylor, meat and poultry suppliers; another from Quinby Company, coffee wholesalers. And then, surprisingly, from a man in the room. His name was Dan Rothschild (known to the trade as Uncle Dan) and he was a supplier of dishes and glassware out of Ithaca, New York. He spoke briefly, saying only that he had confidence in Statler's ability to make a success of the restaurant. When he sat down there was some confusion. The solidarity of the creditors present had been broken and they didn't know quite what to make of it.

The lawyer decided this was the right moment for Statler to speak on his own behalf. A little eloquence from him and the day might be carried. He introduced his client.

Statler did not stand up, he merely leaned forward in his chair for a moment staring at the half-circle of men. There was a touch of belligerence in his look, a lift of his chin, and the men stirred uneasily. Finally he said, "If you men give me a year, every one of you will get every dollar I owe. If you don't, you may wind up not getting one cent."

That was all. The silent room waited for him to continue, but that was all. The lawyer looked at him meaningfully, urging him to say more, but those were all the words Statler had to say. The meeting was over. Finally realizing this, the creditors stood up and left.

Statler turned to Love and said, "Well, how did it go?"

The lawyer shrugged. "You might have given them a little more for their money."

"Damn it, they're business men and they want facts, don't they? If I can give them facts in two sentences, that's a hell of a lot better than giving it in ten."

"We'll see," the lawyer said.

The following day word was received that the creditors had voted to give Statler what he wanted — one year.

"What are you going to do now?" Love asked Statler.

"I'm going to work," Statler said.

CHAPTER 10

THE "EATING OUT" MARKET

The following morning there was a whirlwind of activity at the Statler Restaurant as the boss began to fire people. Not that any of the help was surprised, they all could see the empy tables.

Statler fired the expensive chef imported from New York and hired a cheaper one from Buffalo. He fired his purchasing steward and took on that job himself, rising each morning at four-thirty to appear in the wholesale food marts. He fired his bookkeeper and worked on the books at night. He worked almost around the clock, figuring the meal costs, printing the menus, keeping the books, even taking a shift as cashier. If he could have waited on all the tables, he would have done that.

And all the time business diminished. It was clear that no program of economy, no matter how stringent, could save the restaurant. What was needed was more customers, and the people of Buffalo simply refused to come downtown to eat. The waitresses and bus boys and cooks all knew the restaurant was sinking for the third time, but it seemed that the boss did not know it. They watched in amazement as each day he seemed to work harder, to display greater determination. They began to speculate that perhaps he was a bit off in the head, didn't know what was going on about him. Surely no man in his right mind would hang on so to a dying business.

William Love became concerned about his client's

56

seeming blindness and suggested to him that perhaps the time had at last come for bankruptcy.

"No!" Statler blazed at him. "By God and by damn . . . no!"

"I only want you to face the facts," Love said.

"I *am* facing the facts."

"We must be seeing a different set," Love sighed.

"Very likely."

"What I see is the fact that every day you lose more money."

"What I see," said Statler, "is that every day I have another chance. The time may come when the sheriff locks the door of my restaurant, but *I'll* never lock it. There is one thing I'm damn sure of: no man is ever going to say of me, 'If he'd worked a little harder and held out a little longer, he might have made it.'"

Help came to Statler that summer from a most unexpected source — history. The veterans of the Grand Army of the Republic announced they would hold their annual convention in Buffalo. Statler immediately knew the significance: hundreds of men, women, and children would be pouring into town for a three-day encampment and they would have to eat out, and eat cheaply.

When the G.A.R. veterans stepped off trains and boats in Buffalo the following month they had Statler circulars thrust into their hands by an army of young boys, they faced Statler posters and billboards on the terminal walls, and what they saw they liked — a full course meal for twenty-five cents!

Statler had confidently prepared his restaurant for this flood of business. A turnstile was installed just inside the front door where the customer paid his quarter before entering the dining room. Another turnstile located by the back door let the diners exit without interfering with the people waiting to enter. From the first day of the encampment there was a constant and orderly march of diners through the turnstiles, and the quarters were thrust upon the cashier with such rapidity she had no chance to wrap them. They overflowed the cash drawer and had to be scooped into waste baskets placed around her feet.

By the time the encampment ended Statler had netted several thousand dollars. He was still heavily in debt but now he had some working capital and, perhaps even more important, he had discovered a new weapon to be used in his battle for success — advertising.

During the closing years of the Nineteenth Century the newspaper and periodical advertising was sedate to the extreme. Most of it contained stilted copy and elaborate Victorian gingerbread art. There was as yet little understanding of the power advertising had, not only to sell products but even to alter social patterns.

Statler's first newspaper ad read: "You Eat Downtown? Save time and money by patronizing Statler's Ellicott Square Restaurant. 25 cents. Statler's seats 500."

Within the month Statler discarded that headline and substituted a declarative statement. The ad read: "Eat Downtown!" He denounced the businessmen's habit of going home for lunch as unfair to wives. In later copy he appealed to the businessman's self-interest. "The increase in your business has been brought about by modern up-to-date methods. You can further increase your business upon the same lines. Losing the heart out of your business day by going home to noon luncheon is calculated to increase the business of your competitor who lunches downtown. Let us help you."

Slowly the businessmen of Buffalo responded, partly, no doubt, from the impact of Statler's fear copy. Then they discovered it actually was more convenient to eat downtown, just as Statler had said.

With his weekday business growing, Statler decided

to serve Sunday dinners. When word of this got around, a reporter for the *Buffalo Chronicle* came to interview him. The subsequent newspaper story read:

> In many large cities it is the popular fad for families to go to hotels and restaurants for their Sunday dinners, and Buffalo people are to be given the same opportunity. Beginning next Sunday, Statler, the popular caterer in Ellicott Square, will make a specialty of Sunday dinners, and the same menu and price should make these the most popular meals ever served in the city.

> The first dinner will be served from 12 noon to 2:30 P.M., and the table d'hote dinner from 5:30 P.M. to 8 P.M. Both meals will be served in courses, and the charge for each meal will be 25 cents...Make your preparation to eat "downtown."

There was a good response to this story and Statler learned another valuable lesson — the usefulness of free publicity.

To these business tools he added a third — premium merchandising. Val Sanders, the chef, was surprised one morning when Statler came into the kitchen and handed him five $5 gold pieces.

"Val," Statler said, "I want you to wrap these in waxed paper and put them into five different servings of ice cream." The chef looked at him in disbelief. Statler laughed and said, "No, I'm not crazy. I'm just going to make five people very happy this afternoon. The folks who get the gold pieces are going to talk about it all week. And we may even get a newspaper story about this. It'll pay off in new customers, so don't worry."

Statler promoted the idea in newspaper space advertising, and in trolley car cards, showing a picture of Chef Val inserting the gold pieces into the ice cream. Many of those who came to the restaurant only to be lucky developed the habit of eating there.

Other promotions were devised. All weekday diners were given raffle coupons for a big drawing to be held on Sunday. The holder of the lucky number, *if* he was in the restaurant, received a prize. There were substantial prizes, one time a grand piano and another time a live pony.

The tools of advertising, publicity, merchandising and promotion were crudely used by Statler in the beginning, for there was no body of experience he could learn from. As he refined these tools, as he found what would work and what would not, he created guidelines for the great hotel and restaurant and resort advertising that was to blossom during the Twentieth Century. It was a simple concept: find out what the public wants, give it to them in an attractive package at a price they can afford, and then tell them what you are doing.

The correctness of Statler's approach was proved by his own success. By 1901, six years after the restaurant had opened, he was free of all debt and had a savings account of $60,000. He should have been most pleased.

Perhaps he was pleased, but far from content. He had not forgotten the dream of owning his own hotel, and $60,000 was not sufficient capital to make it reality.

CHAPTER 11

BUFFALO'S PAN-AMERICAN EXPOSITION

Someone said, "Let's hold a fair! It'll put our town on the map!"

No one knows who first said those words, but soon they were being repeated all through Buffalo's business community. It was not an original idea, for America was having a rash of centennial expositions as historic anniversaries rolled around. Philadelphia had started it all with an extremely successful "Centennial of Independence" in 1876 and now, 24 years later, the ingredients of an exposition were pretty well set: they were education, fun and a modest amount of sex.

The fair's boosters and planners included Statler and at one of the early meetings he pointed out that the town did not have sufficient hotel space to accommodate the great crowds that would come to the exposition. He proposed that he build "the world's largest hotel" right next to the fair grounds. It would be a temporary wood structure, and demolished at the end of the fair. Even the most sanguine boosters drew back a bit from this grandiose project. To build the world's biggest hotel exclusively for the fair, for a life's expectancy of six months — it seemed madness!

Little support came to Statler in the beginning, and some of the hotel men in town were openly hostile. They observed that hotel management was an extremely complicated and hazardous art that required considerable training and judgment. Statler was a successful restaurateur, they granted, but his hotel experience was meagre. His critics

61

declared that being a night clerk in a hick town hardly qualified a man to build and operate "the world's largest hotel."

There was logic to their words, as any man could see — any man but Statler. For all his self-training, his careful study of business techniques, he often made decisions by hunch, by intuition, and once he had committed himself to a course of action there was no turning him aside. He listened to the "logic" of his opponents and found it irrelevant. The operative facts were simply these: he was 37 years old and if he was to realize his lifelong ambition to build and operate his own hotel he'd better move soon — in fact, now!

Statler's high reputation in Buffalo as a shrewd and honest man came to his aid and he had little difficulty in raising the necessary money. Some of it was obtained from his old friends in Wheeling, some in Buffalo, and to this he added his life's savings of $60,000. Once more he was going for broke.

The Buffalo firm of Thompson, Hubman and Fisher won the construction contract for a two-story, rectangular structure of 2,084 rooms that could accommodate 5,000 guests. It was to be made of wood, but coated over with a thin layer of plaster so that it would have a solid and permanent look yet be easy to junk at the end of the exposition.

Work began in October, 1900, and the contractors soon discovered there was a problem they had not anticipated — the boss! E. M. Statler was on the job every working hour. He had made his brother William manager of the restaurant and was free to devote full time to the new project. By prodigious study he had taught himself to read construction blueprints and he personally supervised the placement of every board. Not only did he frazzle the contractors' nerves by his demand for perfect workmanship, he frequently changed construction details as he went along, adding innovation upon innovation.

While he expected top workmanship and materials, he also demanded economy, thus squeezing the contractors from both sides. When the electrical subcontractor submitted a bid of $8,000 to install a room-to-front-desk bell system, Statler summoned the man and said:

"You're charging too much for the bell system. Reduce it."

"The hell I'll reduce it," the man replied.

"I know what your costs are, both labor and materials, and I know you'll make a fair profit at six thousand."

"I won't be chiseled," the man shouted.

"And I won't be swindled," Statler replied in the same tone of voice. They glared at each other for a moment, and then Statler said, "Meet my figure or I'll throw out the whole bell system."

"You can't do that," the subcontractor scoffed.

"I can and I have," Statler snapped. "No bell system."

The man looked incredulous. "How is a guest going to summon a bellboy?"

"I don't know," Statler admitted, "but I'll think of something."

And he did. A few days later he said to the general contractor, "I want three little American flags put in a standard in every room. And I want three holes drilled in the outside of each hall door." Then he grinned. "It's my new bell system, and it's better than the old one."

"I don't get it, Mr. Statler."

"There are four miles of corridors in the hotel and when a guest rings down to the desk for service the boy will have to walk a mile in some cases and that takes time. The guest becomes annoyed, thinks that no one is answering his bell. And when the boy arrives and finds what is wanted, he has to retrace that mile to get the ice water, or whatever the order is, and then retrace that mile for the third time. Now, with my new system, I'm going to station a bellboy at each right angle of the corridors so he has a view of an entire wing. When the guest wants something, he indicates what it is by inserting the correct number of flags outside his door and the boy sees it at once. Much faster service. More satisfied guests. Cheaper."

The new system worked just as Statler had predicted. It required 50 bellboys to a shift, but since labor was cheap, and since the newly invented telephone was not in common use, this seemed the perfect solution. The guests were delighted with the innovation and the hotel received much favorable publicity.

"Skippers will be your big problem," an experienced hotel man warned Statler when he first announced his plan. "It's bad enough in a regular house where there is only one main entrance which can be watched by the desk clerk, but in the type of resort hotel you propose to build, and with the kind of people who will be attracted to any exposition, you'll be lucky to collect sixty percent of the room rent that's owed you. They'll move in and out of the place like it was a sieve."

"Hmmmm," Statler mused. "I'll have to solve that problem."

"Solve it!" the man hooted. "That problem hasn't been solved since Adam was driven out of the Garden of Eden."

Solve it Statler did. He did the simplest and most obvious thing — he collected from the guests when they checked in, not when they checked out. The room rates were $2 to $2.50 and the price included three meals a day. When the guest checked in he purchased a ticket entitling him to one week's food and lodging and each time he entered the dining room his ticket was punched. When he checked out he submitted his ticket to the cashier and received a refund for the unused portion.

There were no skippers at Statler's Pan-American

Hotel. Nor were there any scoffers left among the hotel men. In the August 1901 issue of *Hotel Gazette,* a leading trade paper, was this paragraph:

The system at Statler's is fine...bellboy, chambermaid, dining room and office...all perfected. Manager Statler is a wonder...In all the hustle and bustle the hotel has an air that is pleasing. They are never too busy but what a bellboy can be had at once. The cashier is never too busy to change a fivespot. The clerk, room, key or mail, finds time to answer courteously a thousand questions an hour. In the dining room you are promptly waited on and served with good food.

It seemed that the hotel was going to be a financial success, but its destiny was tied to the Pan-American Exposition, which was to be a monumental failure.

The omens were bad from the very beginning. The exposition was half constructed when an early spring wind storm descended upon Buffalo and flattened many of the buildings. A month later torrential rains came and miles of pavement within the Exposition peeled up. The roads were patched in a haphazard manner and the carriage rides, designed to attract the more affluent visitors, became teeth-jolting torture. For many weeks after the gates opened the weather was cold and wet. Even the Eskimos in the Alaska exhibit caught pneumonia; so did many of the Redskins in the "Indian Congress" show. The Hawaiian dancers thought of their sunny homeland and were depressed and lackadaisical in their performance.

The promoters of the Exposition had counted heavily on Niagara Falls to help lure visitors. It did, but not *to* the fair, *away* from it. The average visitor spent a single, bone-chilling day at the Exposition, then took off for Niagara Falls, and from there went home. Statler's Pan-American Hotel, designed to sleep 5,000 guests a night, never had more than 1,500 on any given time.

After a miserable June and July, August arrived with a

blaze of sunshine that thawed out the Exposition. Crowds came in increasing numbers and there was a hope for financial success after all. When word came that the President of the United States, William McKinley, would visit the Exposition in September and hold a reception in the Hall of Music, spirits soared.

The President's special train arrived at the Exposition gates on September 4 to be greeted by a great crowd and a salute of 21 guns. The guns were fired too close to the train and the windows of the front car were shattered. The crowd gasped in horror, but the President stepped out of the train unhurt and made a graceful little joke about the enthusiasm of the gunners. This endeared him to the crowd and a great cheer went up.

McKinley engendered good feeling wherever he went. He was a courtly man who didn't put on airs but moved with natural dignity. He was not a brilliant speaker but an able one. His good will and honesty were beyond question, as was his personal life. He was devoted to his invalid wife, and was an active member of the Methodist Episcopal Church. William McKinley was so respected, so well liked, that it was difficult to conceive of any man wanting to harm him.

The day following his arrival the President and his party visited Niagara Falls. That evening he returned to the Exposition to speak to 50,000 people gathered on the Esplanade. On Friday, September 6, he held a reception in the Exposition's Hall of Music. There was a long, long line of people waiting to shake McKinley's hand, and in the middle of the line was an unobtrusive little man named Leon Czolgosz. One thing did mark him, his right hand was bandaged. No one knew that inside the cumbersome handkerchief bandage was a .32 caliber nickel-plated Iver-Johnson revolver.

The anarchist Czolgosz moved forward a step at a time as the line moved. Finally he was in front of the President.

McKinley noted with sympathy that the man's right hand was bandaged and considerately put out his own left one. At this moment the bandage blazed and two shots ripped into the President, one of them puncturing his abdomen. A Secret Service man jumped Czolgosz but it was too late, the President had been mortally wounded. He lingered a few days but on September 14 he died. For all practical purposes the Pan-American Exposition died with him. Silence filled the gingerbread palaces and exhibitions; the mourning nation was not in the mood for fun and games.

As quickly as possible Statler wound up his affairs at the Exposition. The building was demolished, the furniture sold, the dishes and silver carted back downtown to his restaurant. The proprietor of the "biggest hotel in the world" was again a restaurateur.

To the town's amazement, Statler reported a small profit on his venture. By the most careful management he was able to pay off all the investors and suppliers and employees and still come back downtown with his own savings restored plus a few thousand dollars more. This was not what he had hoped for, still he was about the only concessionaire to come out of the Exposition with his skin intact — no mean accomplishment.

With future projects crowding his mind, Statler solicited letters from some of his contractors and suppliers. Typical of them was one written by C. A. Criqui:

> When Mr. Statler was negotiating to build his large hotel in this city, he was an entire stranger to me, and I met him after bids had been opened on his work. My contract amounted to about $10,000. As payments came due on my work, my requisitions were immediately checked and checks were sent to me without delay.
>
> Mr. Statler is a very cool, conservative, even-tempered, thorough businessman. In so large an enterprise of construction as his was, there is always something to excite and worry an ordinary man. In the times of year in which

CHAPTER 12

"MEET ME IN ST. LOUIS, LOOEY"

"Ellsworth, let's take a vacation."

Statler looked at his wife with an expression of shock; it was as if she had said an obscene word.

"Let's go to Florida for a few weeks," she persisted.

"Florida!" he said, putting into the word scorn and disbelief.

He could, with good conscience, take Canadian fishing trips with his cronies because their dialogue was mainly about business. The fishing pole in his hand did not in any way prevent him from working. But to go to Florida with his wife, to sit stultified in the hot sun while other men were up North having the excitement and satisfaction of conducting their businesses, it was a prospect he found exceedingly painful.

"I just feel I have to get away from the cold and the ice for a while," she said. Then added quickly, "And I don't want to go alone."

Had she posed the vacation as necessary for his sake, she would have lost; posing it for her own, she won. Even so, it was a most limited victory, for they had been in Florida hardly more than a week when Statler received a wire from a David R. Francis who identified himself as the president of a proposed "Louisiana Purchase Exposition" to be held in St. Louis in the spring, summer and fall of 1904. The wire asked Statler if he would be interested in building and operating a temporary hotel inside the

Exposition grounds. He sent back a telegram that read, "Yes." Then he began to pack for the trip to St. Louis.

To the expression on his wife's face he responded defensively, "I didn't tell them I'd do it, I only said I was *interested* in doing it. There were a lot of things wrong about the Buffalo Fair besides poor weather. I'm going to see what St. Louis has planned, and if I don't like it I won't join it."

"I shouldn't think the public would be interested in a second world's fair so soon," she observed.

He grinned at her. "Not much of the public went to the first one."

Upon arrival in St. Louis, Statler found David Francis to his liking. The president of the Exposition was crisp and judicious and capable of patient attention to detail.

"One of the shortcomings in Buffalo," Statler said to him, "was the lack of glamour and mystery."

"That was my impression when I visited it," Francis agreed. "Let me show you our foreign concessions to date."

He handed Statler a paper which listed Mysterious Asia, Ceylon Tea Garden, Siberian Railroad, German Tyrolean Alps, Irish Village, Japanese Village, Chinese Village, Jerusalem, Moorish Palace, Streets of Seville, Paris and France. Another list was titled Educational Exhibits: New York to North Pole, Miniature Colorado Gold Mine, Submarine Diving, Fire Fighting Exhibit, Grant's Log Cabin and Lincoln's Log Cabin.

"It is our theory," Francis said, "that stocking a fair with educational and mysterious and entertaining exhibits is only half the job. They must be advertised and merchandised. We intend to have every single day of the fair dedicated to a different ethnic, geographic, trade, fraternal, social or religious group. If you undertake the hotel, Mr. Statler, we would hope to have it pretty well booked by these groups before we even open our gates."

Statler spent several days with Francis and with Isaac

Taylor, the fair's architect, then announced that he would go home to Buffalo and think about it. He'd give them a decision within the month.

Friends and associates back in Buffalo were horrified when they heard that he was thinking of another plunge into a world's fair. A banker said to him, "E.M., you got out with your shirt last time. . ."

"I got out with a few new shirts as well," Statler countered.

"So you did. But why take another chance?"

"I don't take chances, I take risks. There's a difference."

The banker gave an impatient wave of his hand.

Statler continued, "Life forces risks upon us, even if we sit still and do nothing. I prefer to keep moving and choose my own."

Wherever he went, with whomever he talked, the advice was the same — stay out of the fair. He listened and pondered and then made his decision. He was going in.

On November 2, 1902, he sent his proposal to the Exposition directors:

I am now prepared to make you a definite proposition for a hotel concession inside the Fair Grounds. I will agree to erect not less than a 2,000 room house — plans, specifications and furnishings to be approved by you. For this concession I will agree to pay 25 cents per guest per day in addition to the 50 cents per guest gate admission, same to be paid daily in advance. On all meals and feedings of all nature, bar, cigar and other things sold in the house, I will agree to pay 25 percent of the gross receipts. Building and equipping of such a house as I propose will cost not less than $300,000, and I would have sections of it fitted to take care of the best class of trade, and sections with rooms that would be put at a price within the reach of the masses.

My experience with the 2,100 room house I built in Buffalo, coupled with my financial condition, will enable me to successfully carry out this concession, if granted. I refer you to any or all Buffalo banks and business houses as to my ability and standing. I shall be glad to come on to St. Louis and confer with you if you wish it.

✒ He was summoned to St. Louis and when he revealed he had lined up sufficient investment money, he was given the concession. Under the influence of their mutual enthusiasm, Francis and Statler expanded the original plans. The hotel would cover four city blocks and have 2,257 rooms; 500 of the rooms would have private baths. Two dining rooms would seat 2,000 each and, as a concession to the other restaurants scheduled to open at the fair, Statler's hotel would have both European and American plan. Room rates under the European plan would run from $1.50 to $5.50 and under American plan $3 to $7.

Once the size of the structure was determined, Statler sat down with Isaac Taylor to evolve the architecture. Statler stated his one basic demand — the building's appearance should promise excitement and mystery. All this had to be accomplished within the limits of the architectural style of the period, of course. Isaac Taylor might blaze a new trail, but not one too far from the beaten path or the public might not respond.

In the half-century following the Civil War the nation's architecture was labeled "Victorian," which was actually a medley of many styles — derivative Gothic, some French Renaissance, some English Tudor, all frosted over with balconies, pendants, cupolas, witches' hats and wooden icicles. By the time Statler and Taylor sat down at the drawing table a new influence was insinuating itself — Moorish.

Under Taylor's pencil the facade of the hotel was dominated by two great Moorish towers, crenelated at the top to give the impression that they were occupied by the Foreign Legion which was defending civilization from attack by some unidentified infidels. The building was, perhaps, in questionable taste but it *was* mysterious.

Once inside, the hotel became somewhat less glamorous. The walls were made of wallboard covered over with fireproofed green burlap. Fire escapes on the three-story structure consisted of wooden ladders nailed between each pair of windows. Still, there was something impressive about the sheer size of the place and the numbers of employees needed to operate it. There were 287 waitresses, 150 meat chefs and salad chefs and pastry chefs, 150 bellboys, almost a hundred in maintenance — a total of 1,000 men, women and boys.

The new room service system also caused much comment. Improving on his Buffalo system of flags, Statler had a wooden semaphore placed outside each room door. It was operated by a string that ran through a hole to the room's interior and ended with a small steel ring to be placed on a series of nails. If the semaphore was pulled to an acute angle, ice water was desired; if to a right angle, the bellboy was to knock for instructions.

With the major construction and operating problems solved, Statler turned his attention to advertising and promotion, hiring Fuller and Company of Chicago as his agency.

"I'm giving you $80,000 for advertising," he told Fuller. "If the people come to the Exposition we can afford to spend the money. If they don't, we'll need the promotion badly."

He fully understood the job advertising could and could not do, and the agency people were delighted that they did not have to educate this client. If they thought they had an easy client, they were wrong. Statler was a perfectionist in advertising, as in everything else, and he studied every comma in the copy, wrote much of it himself.

In publicity and promotion he was particularly inventive. "I'm going to call the hotel the Inside Inn. That name alone ought to get us a lot of free space." He was quite right. The St. Louis *Globe-Democrat* published a story at once:

> If the hotel inside the World's Fair Grounds is to be called the Inside Inn, will the one outside be called the Outside Inn, may we ask? And how will those in the Inside Inn get outside, and how will those in the Outside Inn get inside? Or, to put it another way, how will those outside the Inside Inn get in the Outside Inn, or those inside the Outside Inn get in the ... etc., etc.

The story went on for a full column and was picked up by a press syndicate and reprinted through the country. Thousands of prospective visitors to the fair may have had only the vaguest ideas about the exhibits awaiting them, but they were certainly clear about the existence of the Inside Inn.

Statler wrote a platform for the Inside Inn and gave it to the press.

> The policy of this house is to please. No guest will leave the house displeased if concessions will please . . . No employee is to be retained who cannot please guests. Guests are invited to complain and suggest improvements and betterments. A complaint office will be maintained where a competent employee will take down on properly numbered blanks in triplicate complaints or suggestions. No verbal complaints or suggestions received. The rate for one or two or more in a room will be on the door . . . and maintained there at all times. Any room clerk who charges more will be dismissed.

The public, accustomed to the patronizing and often insulting treatment by many hotel staffs, read this story with amazement. They determined to try out this new kind of establishment when it opened and see if the claims were really true.

Not long before the opening date there occurred a major crisis. One of Statler's talents was the ability to remain calm under pressure and to find solutions that excited or angry men overlooked. On this occasion, however, even Statler's talents seemed inadequate.

The contract for the bedroom furniture had been awarded to the Lammert Furniture Company of St. Louis. The order was for two thousand beds, two thousand bureaus, and three thousand chairs. When it came time for delivery Statler didn't have the money to meet the bill. He had made so many costly additions and changes during construction that costs had soared to $620,000 ($100,000 of which was his own life's savings). There was simply no money left to pay for the room furniture and he asked Lammert for 60 days' credit. This only served to alarm the furniture makers and after careful consideration they announced that they would deliver for cash only. Statler conferred with his backers to discover that he had stretched his credit to the utmost limits. Even his strongest admirers were annoyed at his highhanded methods of making expensive changes and they figured he was in a hole that he had dug for himself. They were fearful for the money they had already invested and they were not in the mood to advance any more.

Turn as he might, Statler could find no way out of his entrapment. The opening day of the fair was rushing at him and he had his enormous hotel full of everything but beds. Disaster was but days away. Yet he didn't panic. He turned to his staff a face that was calm if a little preoccupied. He alone remained convinced that there was a solution somewhere. He alone turned out to be right.

He finally thought of the railroads as supplying a possible solution. They were selling reduced rate tickets to the fair and he went to them with the proposal that they extract from the excursionists a ten percent down payment on hotel accommodations. There was no particular reason why the railroads should do this, and several reasons why they should not. It would increase their administrative costs and do nothing to increase sales, might even decrease them. Despite this, Statler got them to do it. With that money he bought his beds.

A few years later a railroad official recalled these events and said, "I'm damned if I know why we bailed Statler out. There was something about the man, I guess. He didn't whine about his troubles, he didn't beg, he simply laid the facts on the table in such a manner that you couldn't help but believe in him. A guy with his kind of guts, well, you felt he deserved a little help."

CHAPTER 13

METTLE OF A MANAGER

The nation's mood in the spring of 1904 seemed to augur well for the Louisiana Purchase Exposition. America was feeling her oats. In 1898 she had won the Spanish-American war after only ten weeks of fighting. The railroads had linked the country together from the Pacific to the Atlantic and the nation's total trackage had reached 200,000 miles, more than was contained in all of Europe. Teddy Roosevelt was in the White House and deciding to dig the Panama Canal. Robert E. Peary was making another assault on the Arctic and promised to "nail the Stars and Stripes to the North Pole." The Wright Brothers had flown a machine in the air. There seemed nothing America couldn't do and she was ready to celebrate. How better than going to the Fair?

Fairs were deep in the fabric of American life, but during the last half of the Nineteenth Century they had fallen into some disrepute. The county fair, which had started out as an agrarian festival with contests for produce and livestock, had more and more taken on the aspect of a carnival. The midway concessions came to dominate the fairs with wheels of chance, freaks, and "Egyptian Dancing Girls" who put on performances for men only.

Protestant fundamentalists denounced the fairs as breeding grounds of drunkenness, debauchery and sin. They may well have been right, but they missed the principal fault — the fairs had become cheap and tawdry. The nation was eager for a fair of beauty and grace, and one was being created in St. Louis.

The French pavilion set the tone with its reproduction of the Grand Trianon. There were 22 other foreign pavilions, each done in the architecture of its native land, and they made a vast and colorful mosaic over 1,400 acres. In addition there were fifteen major exhibition halls to display the technological progress being made by the United States. There were 250 pieces of group sculpture, 1,000 single figures, all installed under the supervision of the renowned American sculptor, Augustus Saint-Gaudens.

Framing the buildings and statuary were gardens of immense size and variety. There was a six-acre rose garden; formal sunken gardens with trimmed boxwood and privet; an enormous floral clock; waterfalls that cascaded into reflection pools; and even a lagoon on which floated gondolas.

As all this took shape during the opening months of 1904 a mood of optimism swept through the staff. Everyone, from the president of the Exposition right down to the plumbers and gardeners, was convinced they were creating the most beautiful fair ever and that the public would respond in overwhelming numbers. Even Statler, not given to wishful thinking, acquired the contagious optimism. It seemed to him that nothing short of some catastrophe could prevent the Inside Inn from being a great success.

The grand opening of the Louisiana Purchase Exposition was scheduled for April 30, 1904. The week prior had been cold and wet, but this day dawned crisp and sunny. "A perfect day for a fair," everyone said. By ten o'clock over 200,000 people had entered the grounds. No fair to that date had attracted such crowds on opening day.

As a major concessionaire, Statler had been invited to join in the opening festivities, but he declined. He had no appetite for the spotlight, nor any need to be in the company of the celebrated. Besides, he had work to do at the Inn.

At 9:45 the special emissary representing President Theodore Roosevelt arrived at the Exposition's Administration Building. It was William Howard Taft, Secretary of War. The parade, led by the Grand Marshal, General Edmund Rice, started off for the reviewing stand at the plaza of the Louisiana Monument. The parade was escorted by the Jefferson Guards (the Exposition police force) and 200 Philippine Boy Scouts. Foreign dignitaries in native clothing came next — the most colorful being the Imperial Chinese Commissioner, Prince Pu Lun. Large delegations of Indian tribes, the original inhabitants of the Louisiana Territory, marched in full regalia. John Philip Sousa stepped out grandly in front of his band while it played a new march, "Louisiana."

St. Louis Mayor Rolla Wells was at the reviewing stand to receive the notables one by one as they mounted the steps to stand at his side. When the last of them arrived, a 400-voice choir sang "The Hymn of the West."

There came the inevitable speeches, but it had been such a grand show this far that the public accepted them with good cheer. Each speaker tried to outdo the preceding ones in hyperbole, the undoubted winner being Exposition President David Francis who threw wide his arms and cried: "Open ye gates. Swing wide ye portals. Enter herein, ye sons of men. Learn the lessons here taught and gather from it inspiration for still greater accomplishments."

At this moment President Theodore Roosevelt in the White House pressed a telegraph key that activated all the fountains of the Fair in St. Louis. Ten thousand flags broke out and snapped in the breeze; water leaped into the air, then cascaded down the esplanade from pool to pool. Topping it all came the heavy booms of a ceremonial cannonade. The Fair was open!

Some distance away, in the kitchen of the Inside Inn, three men writhed on the floor in agony. One of them was Ellsworth Statler.

It had been an extremely busy morning at the Inside Inn as guests by the hundreds arrived to claim their reserved rooms. Shortly after the Inn doors were opened C. H. Shafer, the chief room clerk, had a long line before his desk. It grew longer by the hour until it completely circled the lobby and extended out into the plaza in front of the Inn.

Statler viewed the line with some concern and said to Harry Watcham, the Inn's manager, "This isn't good. I don't like to have a guest wait for his room."

Watcham said, "They understand that on an opening day with a crowd like this . . ."

"They can understand and still be annoyed," Statler said. "Every minute they stand in line for a room, that's a minute away from the Exposition which they came to see. You and I will have to give Shafer a hand."

Statler ordered the bell captain to bring two more desks to the lobby, which he and Watcham occupied. With the waiting line split into three segments the registration and rooming of guests proceeded much more rapidly. By ten o'clock there weren't more than a dozen guests waiting and the registration was keeping pace with the new arrivals.

At about 10:15 a young man wearing a white apron and jacket of the steward's department came into the lobby. His name was Charles Goodrich and he was a coffee boy. When he saw Manager Watcham he went up to him and spoke in a low tone. Watcham nodded and started to stand up.

"What's wrong?" Statler asked from his desk.

"The coffee urn ain't working right, sir," the boy said. "The chef can't fix it?"

"I don't know, sir. But he told me to tell Mr. Watcham."

Watcham said, "I'll go have a look."

"I'll go," Statler said, waving him back to the desk.

When Statler and the coffee boy arrived in the kitchen they joined Chef Louis Rosenbloom before a 50-gallon coffee urn that gurgled and burbled and shot spurts of steam from several pipe connections.

Afer a moment's observation Statler said, "I think the trouble is . . ."

The sentence was never completed, the thought never expressed. With a mighty roar, the side of the urn blew out and fifty gallons of boiling water scalded the three of them.

Statler and Rosenbloom were in almost unendurable agony, the boy was better off — he was unconscious. Statler had taken the precaution of hiring a house doctor for the Inn, but at this moment he was off watching the Fair's opening ceremonies. It was three hours before he could be found and brought back to Statler's room to which the kitchen help had carried him. The doctor found Statler delirious, his temperature 105 degrees. He ordered all three men taken to the St. Anthony Hospital at once. By the time the ambulance arrived, the coffee boy was dead.

The chef was the least burned and was back on the job in a matter of weeks, but Statler lay near death. To the distraught wife the doctor explained, "He had third degree burns on the front of his body from the waist down to his toes. Men have died with lesser burns. His basic good health is a factor in his favor, but . . ." the doctor shrugged slightly, ". . . we'll just have to wait and see."

No pain is more intense, more constant than that of burned flesh, cooked veins and muscles and nerves. Part of the horror was watching the flesh turn black and fall off. Even the medical treatment seemed designed to torture.

Statler's body was bandaged from the waist down,

and each day the doctors removed the gauze which had, over the previous twenty-four hours, soaked up the blood and become adhered to the raw flesh. The doctors worked slowly, soaking the bandages and removing an inch at a time, but however tender their fingers, they were skinning a man alive. Nature did come to the wounded man's aid — most of the time he was delirious.

Mary Statler was at her husband's bedside through each day, returning to the Inside Inn at night to consult with Manager Harry Watcham about any problems that might have come up. There were plenty. The bellboys were threatening to strike, not for more money since tips were plentiful, but for shorter hours. Also, because they were young and it was exciting to defy authority.

The waiters in the European plan dining room (where the diners bought their own meals without relation to room rent) evolved a scheme to make a tidy little profit for themselves. The official procedure provided that the waiters "buy" the food orders in the kitchen, pass a checker, then go on to the dining room where they were paid in turn by the guests. When liquor was ordered the more inventive workers went to the kitchen and poured the whiskey into soft drink bottles, and they were debited by the checker at soft drink prices. When the diner paid them for the whiskey they pocketed the difference.

The various department heads coped as best they could, but in the absence of a strong authoritarian hand to guide it, the whole management machinery of the Inn creaked and staggered and threatened to fall apart. Mary Statler watched in dismay, for she knew that the only hand strong enough to save the Inn lay stricken and fighting for life.

Statler turned his head on the hospital pillow and looked at his wife. His eyes were clouded with pain and opiates but the delirium was gone. She smiled and touched his hand.

"The chef . . .?" he murmured.

"He's all well again."

"The coffee boy?"

"I haven't heard," she lied.

He closed his eyes, exhausted from the effort of speaking. After a few moments he opened his eyes and said, "The house count?"

Each day for the past week she had come prepared for this question and now that it was finally asked she knew that he would live. She replied, "Three thousand four hundred and sixty-five."

He closed his eyes again and tried to translate the house count into dollars and apply them to his indebtedness, but he could not. He had to give his mind over to battling the pain that rose from his stomach and legs in sickening waves.

The following week Mary Statler demanded an opinion from the doctors attending her husband. "He's going to live?" she asked bluntly.

The doctors were cautious. "The prognosis is good," one of them said.

"Is there any reason he can't be taken back to the Inn?" The three men frowned. She persisted. "If we hire a nurse, can't he be treated there as well as here?"

"Mrs. Statler, I must be frank with you," the chief surgeon said. "Your husband is a very sick man and when we say the prognosis is good we do not mean he is out of danger. Nor do we mean that there is a likelihood of complete recovery. I'm sorry to have to tell you, but your husband will never be able to have children. And there is a good chance he may never walk again."

She swallowed with difficulty, but her voice remained under control. "It seems to me," she said, "that a man can get well faster if he's where he's happiest. Near his work. Near the place he's needed."

"He's said this to you?" the surgeon demanded.

"He doesn't have to say it."

"There's a whole series of skin grafts we must do in a few weeks."

"He could return to the hospital for them when it's time," she said stubbornly.

"Let's not make any decision on this for a couple of days, Mrs. Statler."

On the second day the physicians gave reluctant permission and the ambulance returned Statler to the Inside Inn. Those employees who saw him being carried to his room were shocked at his appearance. His face was grey and wasted, without animation, a seeming mask of death.

Within twenty-four hours things began to change in the Inside Inn. It would seem impossible for a critically ill man isolated in an upstairs room to impose his will upon the vast and complicated mechanism of a hotel — but he did. The first manifestations of it was a change in mood. The rather slack atmosphere of drift and procrastination was replaced by alertness and commitment to the job.

Statler set a schedule of daily conferences with his manager and with each department head. To his probing questions they tended at first to lie and cover up, all on the theory that they were protecting him from problems that might further undermine his health. It didn't work out that way, however, for Statler could spot dissimulation before a man was halfway through his opening sentence. His reaction to this sort of charity was so violent that it became immediately evident that it was better therapy to give him the whole truth.

When Manager Watcham reluctantly reported the larceny among the waiters, Statler considered a moment and then said, "Fire them."

"Fire them?" Watcham said with some dismay. "It won't be easy to find two hundred and eighty-seven new men . . ."

"Don't. Hire women. We can find women of good character who will take the job, and in the process we can get some good publicity. Don't try to cover up our problem; announce it honestly and let the public be assured they will henceforth find a genteel and homelike atmosphere in our dining room."

A series of wildcat strikes broke out among the bellboys and no one knew quite how to meet the situation until Statler was brought back from the hospital. He summoned bell captain Richardson to his bedside for a report. He listened and then said, "They have no legitimate complaint about either money or hours."

"I've tried to explain that to them, sir," Richardson replied.

"If that is not the reason for their actions, what is? Do you know? Well, I'll tell you. They're at the age where they want to raise a little hell, that's all. What they need is discipline."

"They do that," Richardson agreed, "but I haven't received any orders . . ."

Statler interrupted. "They tell me you were a sergeant in the Army. That right?"

"Yes, sir."

"Well, damn it, man, get down there and be a sergeant."

"Yes, *sir!*" Richardson grinned, saluting as he left the room.

During June and July Statler received 31 skin grafts, the flesh being taken from his arms to patch his wasted legs. He was shuttled between Inn and hospital without uttering a word of complaint or self-pity. Then came his day of triumph — he could sit in a wheeled chair! With a bellboy supplying motive power, he made an inspection of every corner of his domain. From that day he took personal charge and the Inn quickly achieved smooth efficiency.

In the August 1904 issue of *The Hotel Monthly* the editor gave a report on the Inside Inn. He wrote:

> We expected to find considerable friction in the operating of the Inn, particularly from the fact that it is so big and seemingly unwieldly, but to our surprise we found the house running smoothly and as well ordered as a well run country hotel of a hundred rooms. We found the house clean, the service keyed up in every department. The 287 waitresses in the dining room were under excellent discipline, and we heard from the guests nothing but compliments of their work. There had been severe criticism of the men waiters in the European plan dining room, but these have been dismissed and their places taken by waitresses, with the result that the European plan receipts increased $300 per day right off. The 156 bellboys are under excellent control, and with the signal service... minister satisfactorily to the wants of the guests.

With this kind of publicity the Inside Inn became as big an attraction as any exhibit at the Fair. When the season ended the Inn had grossed $855,986.28. The building was torn down and the materials sold for an additional $30,000. After paying off indebtedness, Statler had made a profit of $361,000.

CHAPTER 14

THE BUFFALO STATLER

Statler came home to Buffalo to find himself a moderately wealthy man. Not only did he have the $361,000 made at the St. Louis Fair but in his absence from town the Ellicott Square restaurant had been running up considerable profits. At forty-two years of age he had come a long distance from the glory hole in the glass factory and many would have envied him his record of business achievement, his position in the community, his financial security. But these were not the things Statler dwelt upon during that winter of 1905. The one fact that preoccupied him was that he was bound to a wheeled chair.

He was a man of action and could not take this affliction philosophically. Pipe and slippers and a good book held no comfort for him. He fretted and glowered until his friends became concerned for him. Duncan McLeod, a poker-playing crony, said,

"Stat, you ought to take it easy. You've got plenty of money."

"Money?" Statler repeated. "What the hell good is that?"

"I mean, you don't *have* to work."

"Good God in heaven! I'd rather be dead than not work!"

"Well, you can manage your restaurant from your wheeled chair."

"Dunc, let's play some poker, huh?"

He gave up trying to explain to his friend that he did

not want to manage a restaurant that was well established and had no problems, presented no challenge. His plans for the future were vague, but they were big. He could not conceive of their being accomplished by an invalid in a wheeled chair.

Since the doctors were dubious about his ever walking, he disregarded them and entered upon his own program of therapy. He heard of the Steuben Sanitarium at Hornell, New York, where he could receive mud baths and massage. He went there and stayed for two months of daily treatments, then he went to Florida to soak up some sun.

One day he said to his wife, "Tomorrow I'm going to walk."

She looked at him in alarm. "Shouldn't we check with the doctors?"

"Do they know how *I* feel, inside me?"

"But . . ."

"Well, *I* feel like I'm going to get out of this wheeled chair and walk. Tomorrow morning!"

He would say no more. She dared not call the doctors.

The next morning he wheeled himself into the middle of the living room, set the brakes, took a firm grip on the chair arms and pushed himself upwards. He stepped out, took one faltering step, then another. He had trouble keeping his balance and the pain brought beads of sweat to his forehead, but he took another step. He headed toward a card table across the room, and when he made it he put his hands on it to steady himself while he turned about. Facing his wife, he retraced his steps. On this return trip he was noticeably steadier and on his face was a triumphant grin. He had escaped his prison!

Two weeks later, without consulting any of his friends or associates, he took off for New York City.

New York was a magnet that worked on most men. What artist felt completely fulfilled without having his work hang in the New York galleries? What architect did not

Mr. Statler, shown in the wheel chair, posed for this photograph with his executive staff.

Mr. Statler opened his first hotel, a highly modern 300-room structure, in 1908. Travelers were provided such hitherto unheard-of luxuries as "a room with a bath for a dollar and a half," telephones, running ice water, and a morning newspaper under the door. When the new 1100-room Buffalo Statler was opened in 1923, the first hotel was rechristened Hotel Buffalo and was operated as a hotel until recently. The present Buffalo Statler-Hilton is that city's major hotel.

BUFFALO HOTELS

THE MOVE
TO BUFFALO
NEW YORK

On July 4, 1895, Mr. Statler opened a 500-seat restaurant on the street floor of Buffalo's Ellicott Square Building, then the "world's largest office building." Pictured below is Statler's inn at the Buffalo Pan-American Exposition of 1901. The assassination of President McKinley doomed the Exposition to financial failure but Mr. Statler managed his inn, designed to sleep 5,000 people, to earn a small profit.

STATLER'S PAN=AMERICAN HOTEL
ONE BLOCK FROM MAIN ENTRANCE.

When dining room waiters were found unsatisfactory, Mr. Statler ordered his manager to hire 287 women to replace them. Waitresses proved to be more courteous and honest. They are pictured at the entrance to the Inside Inn.

ST. LOUIS LOUISIANA PURCHASE EXPOSITION, 1904

Mr. Statler was severly injured by an exploding coffee brewing machine early in the Exposition. He managed the huge Inside Inn first from his hospital bed and later from a wheelchair. He is shown to the right being pushed across the fairgrounds by former Sergeant Richardson, a veteran of the Spanish-American War.

yearn to add his mark upon the New York skyline? What financier did not wish for the power that seemed to go with an office on Wall Street? What social leader did not dream of being part of that magic circle "The Four Hundred"?

For the ambitious man New York was the yardstick by which he measured himself. He either had to submit to such measurement or modify his ambition. Statler went quietly to New York to look for a site upon which he could build his monument — a hotel.

A corner of Sixth Avenue and 40th Street was for sale and it possessed many advantages for a hotel. It overlooked Bryant Park, was near Grand Central Station, and was within easy walking distance of both the Times Square theatre district and the Fifth Avenue shops. Statler bought an option on the property and ordered preliminary plans drawn.

The week the first sketches were delivered to him he received an offer to sell his option at a price that would give him a handsome profit. He sold it, pocketed a profit of $50,000 and returned to Buffalo.

There were both objective and subjective reasons why Statler left New York. First, the city was in the midst of a hotel building boom: William Waldorf Astor had completed his Waldorf Hotel (later to become the Waldorf Astoria) in 1893 and by now it had achieved great social eminence. Its "Peacock Alley" was *the* place to be seen by the great and near-great. In 1894 the elegant Savoy Hotel was built of cream-colored stone on the exterior and light brown marble on the interior. Surpassing both of these in sheer exclusiveness was a hotel about to be built when Statler arrived in town — the Ritz Carlton. Cesar Ritz, a Swiss restaurateur, had built a chain of unrivaled luxury hotels in Europe (Paris, London, Lucerne) and now announced he would build one in New York.

These were not the type of hotel Statler planned; his was to be a commercial house with many service innovations, but the success of the luxury palaces left him uncertain about his future in New York. The mood of the city was bullish, ebulient, extravagent, show for show's sake. In this sophisticated atmosphere he felt an alien, a hick.

There was a group of Wall Street financiers who hung out in William Astor's hotel and was referred to as "the Waldorf crowd." Statler was introduced to them but they refused to take him seriously; they referred to him as "the carnival man." Statler did not need their money, there was plenty available to him in Buffalo and Wheeling, but he found it galling to be patronized. It served to harden his suspicion of Wall Street. He shared with Henry Ford, whom he came to know and admire, a certain financial provincialism. Both men feared that Wall Street was secretly plotting to reach out and take them over.

Despite all these unfavorable factors Statler would no doubt have gone ahead with his plans if his health had been better. When he returned to Buffalo he commented wryly, "They walk awful fast in New York." He meant that both literally and figuratively. The tempo of competition required better health, a faster walk than he now possessed.

Retreat was difficult for Statler, but his business judgment overcame his pride. Years later, when he returned to New York, he was too big and too strong for even the Waldorf crowd to patronize.

Buffalo was delighted to learn that Statler would build his first permanent hotel in their town. There were some misgivings, however, when it was learned that he planned to build his hotel at the corner of Washington and Swan Streets — a rundown neighborhood that was fast becoming a slum.

Buffalo was a "one street town," the street being Main. Land went for $8,000 a front foot on Main Street, whereas land a block away on either side fell off to $1,000 a front foot.

When William Love, his attorney, objected that he was

buying slum lands, Statler grinned and said, "And I'm paying slum prices. It will save us a lot of money we can use in construction."

He paid $90,000 for the property, saving at least three quarters of a million in land cost, and set out to break the "one street town" tradition by building a hotel so unique that it would draw despite the location. And the location was not all that bad, Statler shrewdly judged.

The lot, on which stood the dilapidated old St. John's Church converted to a secondhand furniture store, was close to the best business section at Ellicott Square, and was nearer to the Union Station than any of the existing hotels in town. Statler was not buying a pig in a poke.

For the sixth time in his career Statler invested every cent he had in an new project. He had parlayed the profits from the billard room into the bowling alley and Pie Shop, those profits into the Ellicott Square restaurant; then it all went into the Inn at the Buffalo Pan-American Exposition, into the Inside Inn in St. Louis, and now the sum total of it all was going into a permanent hotel to be built on a slum block. Once again he was going for broke. Yet, such was his reputation that the Buffalo banks unhesitatingly extended him a half million dollars in credit, and would have doubled that amount had he asked for it.

With the financing set, Statler hired the Buffalo architectural firm of Esenwein & Johnson and said to them, "Let's sit down and draw the plans."

He meant quite literally the word "let's," for he knew exactly the nature of the blueprints he wanted. Never had August Esenwein had a more informed, more demanding, more intransigent client with more "wild" ideas. As Statler revealed bit by bit what he wanted him to draw, Esenwein was dismayed and at times even horrified, for Statler was throwing overboard all the traditions of hotel building. What the architect did not then realize was that Statler was in the process of creating new traditions that would shape the manner of hotel construction and operation for decades to come.

"I have in mind a hotel of twelve to fourteen stories and containing about three hundred rooms," Statler said briskly to his architects. "The top floor should contain offices and bedrooms for any members of the staff who may have to spend the night from time to time. The floor below should contain large display rooms for traveling salesmen who carry samples with them. Below that the regular rooms."

Esenwein jotted notes rapidly on a scratchpad.

Casually, almost as an afterthought, Statler said, "Every room is to have its own private bathroom."

The architect's pencil started toward the pad, then paused suspended in mid–air. Esenwein's face held disbelief. "What did you say, Mr. Statler?"

"I said that I want a bath with every room."

"I thought that was what you said. To the best of my knowledge, no hotel in the world has a bath with every room."

"Quite right," Statler grinned, pleased at having disconcerted the architect. "Should get us a lot of publicity, don't you think?"

"A luxury hotel in Buffalo?" Esenwein said. "I'm not at all certain that this town can support one."

"Who said anything about a luxury hotel? This is to be a commercial hotel for traveling salesmen and for families. But it's going to offer the service and comfort and privacy beyond anything ever before offered. I thought up an advertising slogan: 'A room and a bath for a dollar and a half.' What do you thing of that?"

What the architect thought was that Statler had gone out of his mind. He put down his pencil with great deliberation and said, "How you *operate* the hotel is outside my competence, Mr. Statler, but design and construction costs are very much within it. Last month you told me that you wanted this building brought in for under $800,000 and I undertook the job on that basis. But now you announce that you want *three hundred bathrooms!* Do you have any idea how much this will increase costs?"

"Not much," Statler said.

"Not much?" the architect repeated, aghast.

"I got the whole thing figured out. Here, I'll show you."

Statler grabbed the architect's pad and pencil and began to sketch, explaining as he worked. "First off, of course, we eliminate the large public baths that would normally be installed on each floor. In their place we pair off the rooms and their private baths. See, like this. The baths of each adjoining bedrooms would be constructed back to back, with the fixtures and pipes opening into a common shaft. Also, all of them would be vertically stacked so that each pair of bathrooms would be directly above those on the floor below and directly below those on the floor above. Also, each bathroom would have a large mirror over the washbasin which, when removed, would open the interior plumbing shafts to easy access and repair."

Statler went on to explain that besides housing water and waste pipes, the shaft would also carry the heating pipes and the electrical conduits for each room. The architect recognized that as a simple, yet inspired, solution to the plumbing problem. In the years ahead this basic plan was incorporated in all multiple dwelling structures and even in office buildings. The plan became part of the curriculum of all architectural schools and became known as the "Statler plumbing shaft."

Esenwein was delighted with the innovation and impatient to be alone with his drawing board. It was a vain hope, for Statler appeared at his elbow daily to inspect and improve or disapprove.

"It's ridiculous for a guest to have to walk into a dark room at night and have to search for the light cord hanging from the ceiling," he said, "Put a light switch right inside the hall door so he can punch it and have light before entering."

And a few days later: "It's unsightly for the guests to have to look at their clothes hanging from a clothes tree. Put a closet in every room. And a light in the closet."

The following week he said, "I want circulating ice water piped into every bathroom. Ninety percent of the calls for a bellboy are to bring ice water. With ice water already in the room we can cut down on the service staff. Also the guest avoids the annoyance of having to tip the bellboy. And put a telephone in every room so that when the guest does want service, he gets it at once. With a phone at hand the guest will frequently order his meals served in his room. This will help take the transient traffic out of the dining room and make it easier for the townspeople to come and eat. Also the traveling man can communicate easily and instantly with his clients and arrange appointments with a minimum of bother. Once he stops with us he will never again want to patronize a hotel without a phone in the room."

All of Statler's amazing innovations were for the comfort of the guest, to be sure, but also aimed at increased patronage and profits. One day he approached his long-suffering architect with an idea that seemed unrelated to profits or guest comfort or anything else. "I want you to put a large hook beside each bathroom mirror," he said.

The architect said, "Surely, Mr. Statler, that is a frill we can eliminate."

"Not at all," Statler replied. "Without a hook the guests tend to use a face towel just once and then drop it in the basket. With a hook right on eye level he will tend to hang up the towel and use it again. It'll make a great saving in linen and laundry."

The ideas continued to pour out of Statler. "Put a small lamp over each bed so a guest doesn't have to sit up in a chair if he wants to read. Each room must have a writing desk with a pen and stationery carrying the hotel's name and address. Every letter that goes out becomes an advertisement for us.

"Design a mail chute to run to all floors so the guest will not have to descend to the lobby every time he wants to mail a letter. And I want a clock on each floor, too. All upper floor halls should be carpeted wall to wall to deaden the sound of footsteps."

No sooner would a set of preliminary plans be completed than Statler would have a new idea and much of the drawings would have to be done all over again. The harrassed architects began to doubt their wisdom at having taken the job, but they felt excitement, too. They sensed that this building was to make hotel and architectural history.

At last the plans were completed and let out for construction bids. On February 3, 1906 the bids were opened and the job awarded to the Buffalo firm of Mosier and Summers. The cost of building and equipping the 13-story, fireproof building was to be $750,000.

During the two years of construction Statler made effective use of the press, feeding it news items one at a time until he became one of the most widely known (and certainly the most controversial) hotel men in the nation. Typical of the spate of stories was one by John Willy in the trade paper, *Hotel Monthly*:

> E. M. Statler is completing in Buffalo the most remarkable hotel, from serviceable point of view, that has ever been constructed. It represents more new ideas of the utility order than have heretofore been featured under one roof, and many of these ideas are so clever they will doubtless be adopted by other hotel builders and furnishers.

The article listed all the innovations that had previously been publicized, and a new one that Statler had just revealed. Each guest room door was to have an "occupancy indicator which is rigid when the door is locked on the inside, thus avoiding unnecessary disturbance of a guest by a maid or porter. . ." Also there would be ". . . a full-length mirror; and a pincushion with needles and thread and buttons."

The reaction of the other hotel owners in the nation was nowhere near so enthusiastic as the press. Many of them referred to Statler as "that nut in Buffalo." They said that the public didn't want to take a bath every night and that Statler had needlessly increased his construction costs. And as for that slogan, "A room and a bath for a dollar and a half," it might be catchy but such a low rate would lead him straight to bankruptcy.

The hotel was three months from completion when an event took place that gave Statler some wry satisfaction — Wall Street was plunged into a currency panic. Neither historian nor financier was ever quite able to determine the reason, but on October 21, 1907, there began a run on the New York City banks. Vast crowds lined up before the austere institutions and demanded their money which had been on deposit, and in the face of such a run several banks were unable to meet their obligations and temporarily closed their doors.

J. P. Morgan and Carnegie Steel Chairman, Henry Frick, put vast funds at the disposal of the beleaguered banks and saved them. Still there was much dismay along the "Street" and a business recession followed the currency panic. The panic was possible because there was no national banking system (the Federal Reserve System was established in 1913) and each bank had to meet its depositors' demands alone. For this insular reason Buffalo remained practically untouched by the panic.

As he read the news Statler could not help speculating what his position would be if he had stayed in New York to build a hotel with Wall Street money. Beyond a doubt, many of his notes would have been called and he would have faced the terrible ordeal of having to refinance a half-finished hotel in an atmosphere of panic.

Was it luck or foresight that had brought him back to Buffalo? Maybe a little of each, plus a strong loyalty to friends who had helped finance his previous projects. In any event, he was now doubly convinced that Buffalo and Wheeling money was sounder than New York money.

As the hotel took shape, all Buffalo became preoccupied with the process. The hotel was receiving country-wide publicity and Buffalo came to look upon it as almost a civic project, one that had to be admired by all boosters and patriots. When the exterior was finished there must have been a few men and women who thought the structure less than an aesthetic triumph, but no one spoke such heresy. Thousands of citizens trooped by the hotel daily to admire it, and the newspapers ran story after story, each outdoing the previous one in hyperbole.

The truth was, the completed structure was graceless. For all its thirteen stories, the square proportions made the building look squat. The exterior walls were covered with glazed terra cotta tile that carried swirls of color, mostly reds and browns. The thirteenth floor was circled with a crust of lancet arches and the whole thing gave the impression of being a giant cake in which the ingredients had been imperfectly mixed by an apprentice baker. But Buffalo loved it.

Two days before the opening Statler gave the press a preview tour. What the reporters found on the main floor was a lobby, a bar, and two dining rooms so ornate as almost to defy description. There was no single decorative period, but bits of all periods. Wood, glass, marble and plaster were used in lavish and unlikely ways. It gave the impression of being a Cecil B. DeMille movie set.

This was not the way the Buffalo press saw it, however. Typical of the news coverage was a feature story in the *Buffalo News*:

Its artistic exterior of terra cotta... (gives) but a faint idea of its magnificent interior of sumptuous furnishings and pleasing decorative work... The main lobby is built of Italian marble, its stately columns and walls being strikingly handsome while the new kind of chandeliers, of dull iron wrought in fantastic shapes, give the effect of a grand salon... Embedded in the wall facing the front entrance is a huge electrically controlled clock supported, as it were, by two cherubs in kneeling posture... The public dining room is of regal magnificence. The walls contain immense panel paintings made especially for the Statler Hotel... The paintings are of landscape effect, with the oddness and unusual in them which gives a fair idea of the paintings of old, where patriarchs dreamily sat in gilded chairs placed in flower-scented gardens, entrancedly listening to the strains of the harp and lute in the hands of beautiful maidens with flowing tresses and plump shoulders.

Grotesque and fantastic decorative work on the walls and pillars of the dining hall serve to make it attractive. It is lighted by the subdued electric lights hidden beneath colored glazed glass, shedded from the interior of the columns and walls. The solid wall is covered with a deep border of grapevine terra cotta while the rest of the wainscoting is nine feet high, in pure mahogany... In one corner is the orchestra balcony, where sweet strains of music will issue from a bank of tall palms hiding expert musicians.

While the cafe is elaborately finished in elegant style, the elegance of the substantial and unostentatious palm room is the real gem. When the lights are turned on the effect is stunning. The room has a huge dome done in work of the outdoor grapevine effect. In the center of the dome is suspended a beautiful electrolier of dazzling brilliancy. Clusters of electric lights, bursting from flower-effect terra cotta, the lights being draped in artificial grapes and leaves, enhance the beauty of the room.

The walls reaching to a mezzanine floor are of stucco finish, with paintings here and there to give it the luxuriance of the private home of a regal monarch. There is a fountain in the palm room which will be a catchy feature. Standing out from the walls are three miniature dragon heads, each spurting a stream of water, which falls into a basin, beautifully worked, and into three large electric lights, which will be submerged in the water. An arrangement which Mr. Statler is thinking of is to have sweet scented waters sprayed from this fountain, which will cause a perfume to permeate the atmosphere.

The prose did justice to the decor.

The grand opening was scheduled for six o'clock on the evening of January 18. Three hundred guests, the town's civic, political, industrial and social leaders, were invited to a banquet. Shortly before the hour private carriages began to arrive at both the Washington and Swan Street entrances to deliver Buffalo's elite. The ladies were dressed in the height of fashion. Bodices of lace were trimmed with velvet ribbon, the skirts cascaded down in series of flounces to touch the floor and reveal only a peek of a pointed satin slipper. The coiffures were stunning; the long hair piled high and held in place with yarn to form the new "psyche knot." On top of it all was perched precariously a display of egret feathers.

As bewitching as the ladies were, on this evening they were not the center of attention — they were upstaged by a building. Heard on all sides were exclamations of amazement and admiration. Statler, with his wife and mother at his side, was a proud man. Also, he was a man with a surprise for his guests.

When the banquet was about over and waiters were removing the dishes, Statler rose from his chair and walked out of the room. There was mild speculation among the diners that some crisis in management probably needed his attention. He returned within a matter of minutes, however, and in his arms he carried a sixteen-month-old baby boy.

His face beaming, Statler called out, "I want you all to meet my adopted son. His name is Milton but I call him Honey Boy."

There were laughter and applause. After a few minutes of display the child was taken off to his thirteenth floor nursery. Here was a fine human interest story and the reporters begged permission to accompany Honey Boy upstairs and look at the nursery. Permission was given.

On the following day the *Buffalo Courier* reported:

> The room ... occupied by "Honey Boy" is one of the most expensively furnished and finished rooms in the building. "Honey Boy" has his own swimming tub, telephone, bathroom and numerous other conveniences.

All his life this child was to have "conveniences" thrust upon him; the convenience of yachts and motor cars, of big rolls of money in his pants pockets. He was to be spared the burden of hard labor, and thus deprived of the element that might have fused him into responsible manhood. This slow crippling was done to him by his father through the confusion of love.

Part of the financing promised Statler by his backers was $150,000 operating money to be used immediately after the opening. The hope was that this amount would sustain the hotel until it became popular enough with the traveling public to operate in the black. The money was never used because the hotel was immediately successful and profitable. Its uniqueness drew people from all parts of the country, and it educated the traveling public to demand a bath with every room. Hotel men who had scoffed at Statler now followed his lead— they put in baths and closets and bedlights and mirrors and stationery. They had to in order to stay in business.

As the nation's great and near-great came to Statler's hotel he developed a keen publicity sense. Some years later he was to be among the first hotel men to hire a permanent public relations staff, but now he did the job himself. He cultivated friendship with the newspapermen, was generous to them with food and spirits, and never tried to con them, never asked them to create a story where there was none. As a result they trusted him, and they mentioned his hotel whenever possible.

Two weeks after the hotel's opening Statler was leafing through the pile of advance reservations to discover that William Jennings Bryan would be a guest on February 12 and 13. He immediately notified the press. Bryan was newsworthy wherever he went, he was one of the giants of the age, and he was coming to Buffalo to confer with the Erie County Democratic Committee as part of his campaign to win a third Democratic nomination to the Presidency of the United States. The reporters would have swarmed around him whether Statler had called them or not, but the hotel man had a special angle.

There remained across the country, especially in the Mid-West, a body of opinion that held hotels to be dens of sin and debauchery. Statler reasoned that if it became known that Bible-quoting, religious fundamentalist William Jennings Bryan had stayed at his hotel it would be a strong blow against that prejudice.

When Bryan arrived he was put in the best accommodations, the Thomas Jefferson Suite, and given the most meticulous service. When he checked out the following day the reporters met him in the lobby and interviewed him about politics. Then one of them asked the question Statler had been hoping for:

"Can you tell us, sir, how you liked the hotel?"

Bryan thought a moment, then pronounced, "The

Thomas Jefferson Suite is one of the handsomest suites I have ever occupied . . . I compliment Mr. Statler very highly."

Since several million people (including Mr. Bryan) were convinced that Bryan always spoke in the Lord's Name, Statler's hotel seemed to have received His imprimatur.

CHAPTER 15

FAMILY AND FRIENDS

As money rolled in, Statler was constantly urged by his friends to spend some of it on himself. This was difficult because there was little in the way of creature comforts he wanted. Relax, they said, stop working so hard and enjoy yourself; yet his greatest joy was in his work. He did turn increasingly to golf and poker but not with an attitude that could be called relaxing. He approached these games with the same fierce competitiveness he gave to business.

In an old canvas golf bag he carried three clubs — brassie, mashie and putter — and he played for one dollar a hole. No matter what his score (usually in the 90's), if he lost a dollar on the round he would mutter darkly and plot revenge. He seemed to see the money as a measurement of his game.

His poker cronies included Dunc McLeod, a hotel man from Buffalo; Frank Hinkley, a newspaper reporter on the *Buffalo Commercial;* Charles Mosier, the general contractor who built his hotel; William Cowan, a commercial printer and a political power in Buffalo; and Louis R. Davidson, an industrialist.

The poker games sometimes ran through the night. They were certain to do so if Statler was the loser, for he would badger his friends into continuing play to give him a chance to break even. He allowed nothing to disrupt his intense concentration or to slow the game. Once

McLeod won a pot and it was then his turn to deal. He pulled in the chips and began to count them.

"Damn it, Dunc," Statler growled, "count your chips on your own time. Get the cards dealt."

Davidson owned a boat named *Riette* and several times a month they boarded her for a cruise to the Thousand Islands which lay in the throat of Lake Ontario. Statler supplied the food and liquor, and brought a young busboy named Peter Gust Economou to act as steward. Peter was a Greek who could barely speak English but had such charm and eagerness to please that the language problem seemed to disappear. Years later Peter Gust became one of Buffalo's leading restaurateurs and civic leaders.

Statler finally consented to buy an automobile, a large and expensive Marmon, and he hired a chauffeur named John. He drew the line at sitting in the back seat and at putting a uniform on John. When the two of them rolled through the streets of Buffalo sitting in front side by side, John brisk and dapper, Statler slouched and wearing a battered hat, it was difficult to tell which man was the rich one.

When personal competition was not involved Statler became increasingly generous. The Lafayette Presbyterian Church was one of the beneficiaries; he bought the church the largest and finest organ in the city. He chartered a boat, the *North Wind*, to be used for all-expense-paid employee outings, which he always joined. The presence of the boss did not inhibit the party, it enlivened it. "Well, what are we here for?" he'd call out, and that would be a cue for the band to strike up and everyone dance. Statler was an excellent dancer before his legs had been burned, but he was still able to take a whirl around the decks with the waitresses and chambermaids. If the help thought that this intimacy gave them license to slack off a bit on the job, they soon found how wrong they were. In Statler's mind, work was work and play was play, and each should be performed with concentration and efficiency.

McLeod said to Statler one day, "E.M., you ought to build yourself a home."

"What in hell for?" Statler demanded. "I can't get any better service than I do right here in the hotel."

"I wasn't thinking about you, but the baby. A hotel is no place to bring up a child."

"It's not?" Statler asked in surprise.

"No, it's not. A child should have a backyard with grass and trees and birds. He should be able to get himself dirty — with good mud, not with dust. He should have neighbor kids to grow up with."

"Well, I'll think about it, Dunc."

A week later Statler said to his wife, "Mary, a hotel is no place to bring up a child. I'm going to build us a house. What kind of a house would you like?"

She thought a moment and then said, "When I was out in California everything was very nice. I think I'd like to have a California-type bungalow."

"A California bungalow you'll get!" he exclaimed.

Statler threw all his energy and imagination into this new project, and when it was completed, in the middle of four acres on a street named Soldiers Place, it was like no California bungalow anyone had yet conceived. The unique structure was, perhaps, ahead of its time. A decade later, when Hollywood was at its flamboyant best, many a movie star built a "California bungalow" not unlike the structure in Soldiers Place.

The house was rambling and three stories tall, topped by a flatly pitched roof. The third floor was devoted to children's and servants' quarters; the second floor contained a half-dozen bedrooms, each with bath; and the ground floor held a grand entrance hall, a ballroom, two dining rooms, and various sunrooms and parlors. In front of the house was a lagoon stocked with fish and swans.

105

A final Hollywood touch was the installation of an organ in the entrance hall. Statler hired an organist full-time to play the instrument. True, the musician was given other small jobs to do around the house, but he was expected to be available to play the organ at any hour.

"When I want music, I want music," Statler explained to his friends defensively.

He was learning how to spend money.

All this was done in the name of creating a proper environment in which to raise a child, all aimed at making little Milton a regular American boy. When Milton and his governess were installed in the top floor suite he had, in effect, simply moved from a large hotel to a small one. True, there was a yard in which to play but always under the supervising eye of a servant. As for playmates, the neighboring children soon found the regimen surrounding the little rich boy much too restrictive and they came to visit less and less; finally not at all except on formal occasions, such as Milton's birthday when they received presents grander than any they gave.

CHAPTER 16

THE CLEVELAND STATLER

As a playboy Statler turned out to be pretty much a failure. He proved that he could spend money quixotically, flamboyantly, but he could never achieve that easy idleness that marks a hedonist. No matter how many poker games, or golf games, or cruises on the Great Lakes, he remained full of dammed up energy which he just could not discharge in play.

His primary interest remained his hotel, and he kept tinkering with it, adjusting and polishing it, trying to achieve perfection in accommodation and service. He made Frank Hinkley the manager and one day said to him, "I want you to put a pincushion with needle and thread and pins in every room."

"What on earth for?" Hinkley asked.

"For loose buttons, damn it, what do you think for? If a guest has need of small repairs, I want him to be able to take care of it himself if he desires, and not have to bother looking for a tailor."

A week later Statler said to his manager, "Hinkley, I want our guests to receive the morning newspaper free of charge. Shove a copy under the doors each morning."

A few days later Statler marched into Hinkley's office and said brusquely, "I thought I gave orders to have the morning newspaper shoved under each bedroom door."

"We couldn't do it, Stat. The papers are too thick to fit under the door."

"Well, then, cut an inch off the bottom of the doors so the paper will go under."

For a moment Hinkley was disbelieving. "All the doors?" he asked.

"All the doors," came the reply.

"All three hundred of them?"

"All three hundred of them. And get the carpenters started on the job today!"

The Buffalo hotel was Statler's pilot plant, his research laboratory, but there came the time when there was nothing more to be done to it and he had to look elsewhere for challenge.

Once more he cast longing eyes toward New York, but again he hesitated. There was still some country boy in him, still some diffidence before the smooth talkers of Manhattan. While he thought about it a letter came from a committee of civic and industrial leaders in Cleveland, Ohio. The letter said that Cleveland was in need of a first class hotel and invited Statler to come and discuss the possibility of his building one there.

He tossed the letter triumphantly into the air. "They came to me!" he cried. "They want a first class hotel and they didn't go to the New York crowd . . . but to me!" He packed his bag and took the next lake steamer to Cleveland.

The situation there was not exactly as Statler had anticipated. All the business and civic leaders were united in a desire for a hotel, and for Statler to build and operate it, but they had their own ideas as to what kind of a hotel it should be. They wanted an elegant hotel, one that would serve as a social center for Cleveland society. They were eager for Statler to incorporate all his engineering and service innovations, they were even willing to set aside a portion of the house for low-cost rooms to serve the traveling man, but they wanted the public rooms to be of grand dimension and luxuriously furnished. They said quite frankly that they wanted none of his Buffalo decor.

THE CLEVELAND STATLER

Statler listened and pondered and walked the streets looking for location. The real estate brokers showed him sites only on Superior Avenue, for Cleveland, like Buffalo, was a one-street city. Statler had successfully defied that tradition in Buffalo and he refused to be bound by it in Cleveland.

Among the civic leaders he interviewed was James P. Dempsey of the law firm of Squire, Sanders & Dempsey. Dempsey took him to lunch at the exclusive Union Club. Characteristically, Statler came directly to the point.

"The three most important elements in any hotel's success are location, location, location."

Dempsey pulled thoughtfully at his lower lip. Statler took the gesture to mean disagreement and he snapped, "Dempsey, you're a lawyer and I would not presume to tell you how to draw a legal brief. Likewise, I do not expect you to enlighten me on hotel management."

A slow grin spread over Dempsey's face and he said, "I had heard that you're a blunt man. I like that. Easier to do business."

"Quite right," Statler grinned back. "Now then, let me tell you what I've been thinking. Cleveland is going to grow enormously in the next few years. It's going to become too big and too prosperous to have its first class business area confined to one street."

"I quite agree," Dempsey said.

"Any new hotel should be built on the street of the future. Do you have any opinion as to which street that will be?"

"I should say Euclid," the lawyer replied.

"Exactly my conclusion," Statler said.

Dempsey pointed out the window. "See that site on the corner of Euclid and Twelfth? It's owned by Charley Pack, a past-president of our Chamber of Commerce and a booster of the new hotel idea. I think he'd give you a good price."

Statler abruptly pushed back his chair and stood up. "Let's go talk to Pack."

"But we haven't had our lunch," Dempsey exclaimed.

"Hell's fire, we can have lunch any time. Let's go tie down that corner." He was halfway out of the dining room by the time Dempsey got to his feet.

The lawyer was right about Charles Pack; he made the land available at a fraction of its real worth. Statler received a ninety-nine-year lease at an annual rental fee of only $32,500, "without reappraisal or re-evaluation."

Such was Statler's reputation that the financing presented no problems. In a press interview Statler said, "I am incorporating The Statler Company with a capitalization of three million dollars. A million and a half will be in preferred stock and the other million and a half in common . . . As this is a Cleveland enterprise, we do not want Buffalo to furnish all the capital without giving Cleveland citizens an opportunity to secure an interest. Nor do we want to dispose of the stock to a few persons; we prefer about fifty small subscriptions, in amounts of five and ten thousand, in order to give the greatest number an actual interest in the hotel."

Within days the stock was over-subscribed.

Since the hotel was taking on the aspect of a civic enterprise, Statler employed local firms wherever possible. However, he had old loyalties to suppliers which he would not break. He bought silver only from International Silver, and dishes only from Syracuse China. These firms stood by him when he almost went into bankruptcy with the Ellicott Square Restaurant, and his gratitude was to endure a lifetime.

Other services and skills he bought in Cleveland. The outstanding architectural firm of George B. Post & Son was retained to design the building, and the working architect, W. Sydney Wagner, began the sometimes abrasive but always exciting task of collaborating with Statler.

Interior decoration posed a problem. Statler felt sure of his own judgments in all phases of hotel construction and operation except for interior decoration. He wanted his hotels not only to be comfortable but also to have some elegance. This was a decade when America was discovering Old World art and culture, and the wealthier homes proudly displayed at least one European antique chest, or vase or tapestry. Statler wanted such status symbols for his hotels, but he had not the least idea where to find them or how to choose if he did. Also, he had a horror of being victimized by an importer, made a fool by purchasing something worthless.

Cautious questioning in Cleveland brought the unanimous opinion that the outstanding decorator in town was Louis Rorimer, president of Rorimer-Brooks Studios. Rorimer, born and raised in Cleveland, had gone to Europe for his education in art, studying at *Des Arts Decoratifs* and *Academie Julian* in Paris, and at the *Kunstgewerbe* in Munich, Germany. He returned home to teach sculpture and design in the Cleveland School of Art. He went on to become a civic leader, the president and trustee of the Cleveland Playhouse, patron of art festivals and, of course, president of his own highly successful firm of decorators. He was three men in one: artist, teacher, businessman.

Statler felt a reluctance to approach Rorimer because he feared getting involved with temperament. It seemed to him that an interior decorator, by definition, was emotional and unreasonable. Finally he heard an anecdote about the decorator that was reassuring.

When the young Rorimer returned from Europe he undertook to teach a class in architectural modeling and design. When he first entered the modeling room he found he was not much older than the students, and it became immediately clear that they had decided to test his authority. As he walked across the front of the room a ball of soft clay came whizzing through the air, struck him on the left cheekbone and flattened against his face. He reached up and peeled it off, looked at his class a moment, then said with complete self-possession, "Gentlemen, this is not a class in practical politics, so we'll refrain from throwing any more mud. Besides, it's a poor way of molding anything, even opinion."

When Statler heard the story he chuckled and said, "Tell Rorimer I'd like to meet him."

When they met, Statler beheld a man of thirty-eight years with a square, rather fleshy face and a firm chin. Through steel-rimmed glasses he observed the world with both curiosity and equanimity.

"Rorimer, would you care to bid on the job of decorating my hotel? Before you answer, let me tell you it will be a competitive bid. I'm inviting four other decorators to draw up plans and costs for one guestroom. If you enter the competition and don't win, I'm not paying you for your time. You gotta undertake this on your own."

"That's quite customary, Mr. Statler," Rorimer smiled. "I'd be delighted to enter the competition."

By the following month all the competing designs were in Statler's hands and he again summoned Rorimer. "I like what you've got here," he said, waving Rorimer's water color, "but, my God, man, you want as much to do one room as a whole floor cost in my Buffalo house."

"Yes, I've been in your Buffalo hotel," Rorimer replied quietly, "and it does give that impression."

Statler looked up sharply, trying to decide if he had been insulted. Then he laughed and said, "All right, damn it, so I'm not a very good decorator. That's why I'm hiring you. So get on with the job."

Thus began a business relationship that was to last to Statler's death. Rorimer decorated all the Statler hotels subsequently built, as well as Statler's two homes. He imported thousands and thousands of dollars worth of European art treasures for the lobbies and public rooms of the hotels, and no one dared question his decisions to Statler. He eventually became a director in the company, and the only one who could say no to the boss and make it stick.

Rorimer's association with Statler made him wealthy and famous, but these were secondary to a greater satisfaction. He saw in the hotels a chance to educate and elevate the American cultural level. He made each lobby something of a museum, exposing the traveler, perhaps for the first time, to excellence in art. He was not entirely abandoning his role as teacher.

On October 26, 1910, the citizens of Cleveland learned some details of the projected hotel through a story in the *Cleveland Plain Dealer*. The hotel would be sixteen stories high with 800 guestrooms and 800 baths. The cost would be $2,500,000. Statler was quoted:

> The hotel will be a sensible, practical establishment for the traveling public ... It will also be a desirable hotel for fashionable people, with the charm and exquisite harmony found in such houses as the St. Regis in New York.

A hotel for *fashionable* people! A hotel like the *St. Regis in New York!* Those were Statler's words? They were his all right, and they pointed up a basic conflict in his conception of hotel keeping. As the American cities grew and prospered they were demanding elegance and sophistication in their public accommodations. No hotel that did not cater to the middle and upper classes, did not have nightclubs and ballrooms, could hope to prosper. All this drove up the price of the rooms, which was painful to Statler because of his deep emotional commitment to the welfare of the ordinary traveling salesman.

He resolved this by simply having his cake and eating it. Louis Rorimer was given free hand to achieve elegance in the public rooms and the suites; at the same time Statler set aside a block of low priced rooms (with baths, of course) for the traveling men. Room clerks were warned that as long as the cheaper rooms were vacant they were not to pressure a man into the higher priced ones. If a man had a reservation for a cheap room and none was available when he arrived, he was to be given expensive accommodations, even a suite, and still be charged the rate for the room he had reserved.

It was no longer possible to offer "a room and a bath for a dollar and a half," but Statler was determined to do the best he could. After the Cleveland house had been open for a year and it was clear that he could not accommodate all the traveling men who wanted to stay there, he bought a plot of adjacent land and constructed a new wing which contained 300 low priced rooms.

The grand opening of the Cleveland Statler Hotel, which was a charity ball, took place on the evening of October 18, 1912. Hundreds of the town's leading citizens walked through flower bedecked halls to enter the grand ballroom. The *Cleveland Plain Dealer* reported:

(The area was) ... solidly banked with hedges of flowers — more cut flowers, probably, than had ever before decorated a single room in the city.

Statler was pleased by the *Plain Dealer's* account of the opening, but he knew that the hotel trade press would be less dazzled by cut flowers and he waited most impatiently for their reports. John Willy, editor and publisher of the influential *Hotel Monthly*, devoted almost an entire issue to the opening. After giving detailed and glowing accounts of the public rooms, of the decor and the service, he wrote:

Mr. Statler's genius is both creative and adaptive, and is combined with a shrewdness in selecting utilitarian features. He also combines the traits of the dreamer with those of the man of action. His dream castles have materialized ... in such a way as to have given him first place in America as the builder of hotels on original lines.

THE CLEVELAND STATLER

Statler has never kept hotel in New York but he knows the hotels of New York, and of every city of consequence in America. He has traveled from coast to coast investigating the big things and the little things in hotel construction, mechanical equipment, decoration, furnishing and management. Statler is the greatest hotel man in the United States ...

CHAPTER 17

THE DETROIT STATLER

After his success in Cleveland, Statler was besieged by cities that wanted a Statler Hotel. All he had to do was to name a town, any in the country, and all the financing would be immediately pledged. There were two cities that especially wooed him — Pittsburgh and Detroit. Andrew Mellon, whose father had made a fortune in oil and Pittsburgh real estate, headed up a civic movement to get Statler to take over the ailing William Penn Hotel. He was offered carte blanche; he could remodel the hotel, or tear it down and rebuild.

Detroit had as its spokesman a political and civic leader, an ex-postmaster named Homer Warren. He was a large, ruddy-faced man with a booming laugh and a deep baritone singing voice. He liked people with an easy and uncomplicated emotion, and the people could not help liking him in return.

He first achieved prominence in the city during the Spanish-American war when he sang a series of concerts at the Belle Island bandshell. His favorite and closing number was always the song "The Sword of Bunker Hill." At the final note men always cheered and threw their hats in the air, and the ladies wept patriotic tears.

In his office atop the Buffalo hotel, Statler studied the various offers and then purchased a railroad ticket to Pittsburgh and a boat passage to Detroit.

Before his day of departure he signed adoption papers for a baby girl. He named her Marian and took her home to the top floor nursery at Soldiers Place. His parting words to the governess were, "She is to have the best of everything."

The following day he called his staff together (also some reporters) and flipped a coin into the air to determine whether he took the train or the boat. The half dollar spun upward and then down to fall in the palm of his right hand. He slapped it over onto the back of his left hand and looked at it.

"I'm taking the boat ride," he announced with a grin.

The story made fine newspaper publicity, even though a few skeptics pointed out the fact that Statler had not revealed before the flip which city had the heads and which one the tails. Statler had, they guessed, decided upon the Detroit visit long before pulling the coin from his pocket.

The boat sidled up against the pier in Detroit, made fast to the great iron bitts, swung its gangplank out and down. Before the plank was lashed into place a large man leaped upon it and bounded aboard. It was Homer Warren. When he found Statler he began to pump his hand with vigor. They made an incongruous pair. Statler's five feet six inches was dwarfed by Warren's six feet two inches, and the larger man smiled and gestured and talked with such vitality that he seemed about to sweep the smaller man off his feet. It was but a momentary illusion, for there was within the half-smiling Statler an unyielding stiffness. He was polite, but on guard. He was not going to be sold anything — he might buy, but he would not be sold.

"Detroit is going to grow and grow," Warren boomed as he drove his Model T automobile toward the business section. "We're going to be a million people within a few years. You know why? Because we've got Henry Ford. He's figured out a new manufacturing method — the assembly line. He's gonna standardize and mass produce his car faster and cheaper than any of his competitors. There's gonna be the biggest damn expansion of heavy manufacturing this country has ever known, and Detroit is gonna be right in the middle of it, because we got Henry!"

There was a moment of judicious silence between them, then Warren said, "There's a plot of land I want to show you. It may seem to you a bit out of the way at first, but I'm convinced it's in a coming part of town. The main business area is now south of Grand Central Park, but it's gonna move north in the next few years and your hotel would then be in the new part instead of the old part."

The land was on the corner of Washington Boulevard and Bagley Avenue, and was owned by Arthur Fleming, a prominent Detroiter who was anxious that his city have a Statler Hotel.

Statler spent the afternoon examining the area both north and south of the Park and then said to Warren, "Let's go talk to Fleming."

As they climbed into the high black car, Warren looked at his guest and said, "Funny thing, Statler, you and Ford kinda look alike."

In fact, they were more alike than Warren could have possibly guessed. Both were born in the same year, 1863, and to farm families. Neither man had more than minimal education, but both possessed a strong native intelligence and the appetite for work. Both were short of stature and of wiry build. Both had visions of service to the common man; Statler with his room and bath for one dollar and a half, Ford with his $500 automobile. Both were provincials who mistrusted and feared Wall Street.

Both men felt that the fame and wealth that came to them imposed a social responsibility. The month before Statler opened the doors of his Detroit hotel, Henry Ford made the announcement that his minimum wage was to be boosted to an unheard-of $5 for an 8-hour day. Also, he promised his workers a profit-sharing plan. Statler, too, devised a profit-sharing plan that allowed many a maid and bellboy to eventually retire with dignity and security.

As his industrial empire grew, Ford was given to proclaiming little homilies: "Chop your own wood and it will warm you twice." Statler began to publish a house organ in which he urged upon his employees the simple virtues of honesty and thrift and service.

Statler and Ford became friends during the next few years. They were never social intimates but enjoyed a casual, business sort of friendship. Ford frequently ate at Statler's hotel; Statler often visited Ford's factory where he was fascinated with the assembly line techniques, studied them for any applicability to his hotels. He discovered that Ford, like himself, had difficulty in delegating authority and attempted to make all the decisions on all levels.

Statler never stopped learning, never stopped innovating, and he remained far ahead of his competition. When he was planning his last hotel in Boston just before his death, he angrily threw a set of blueprints across his desk to the architect and exclaimed, "This is just like our other houses. Have we run out of ideas? Have we lost all imagination? I don't want this hotel to be as good as the others, I want it to be better! Hell's fire, let's sweat a little!"

The construction of the Detroit hotel began in January 1914 and by the same team that had built the Cleveland house: George B. Post & Sons, Louis Rorimer, Charles Mosier and Ellsworth Statler. The formal opening was on February 6, 1915, and was one of the memorable social events in Detroit's history.

The *Detroit News Tribune* reported that 500 out-of-towners had come to Detroit to be present at the opening of "Mr. Statler's third and most magnificent establishment." All the press, out of town as well as local, gave the most glowing accounts of the opening, and the reporters dogged Statler's footsteps all evening to pick up colorful copy.

One reporter wrote:

When we arrived at the Hotel's main entrance shortly before 6 o'clock that night, we found a great crowd of people, who wanted to see the city's new show place, already semi-blocking the door. But for us the Royal Press Suite had been reserved — the 150 men of the press were guests of E. M. Statler and the fray soon started.

Another newsman reported:

Five hundred people crowded into the hotel to eat and to admire. There were so many of them that the formal banquet was served in three sittings. Those not engaged in eating made inspection tours of the building. Women in evening dress edged gingerly past the kitchen ranges. Ballrooms, service departments, everywhere the sight-seeing crowd jostled and gaped ... (Statler) trotted about the house, anxiously concerned that (his guests) ... see and appreciate. He pointed out to sight-seers a hook in the middle of the bathroom door. "To hang your pajamas on," he explained. "I can never find a place to hang my pajamas in other hotels, so I put one on every bathroom door in this one."

Another paper headlined:

The Roosevelt of Hoteldom. His neck outthrust, his ... head lowered as though he was prepared to butt down a stone wall, his ready-made coat flying behind him — he ran up and down flights of stairs, transversing miles of back alleys in those fourteen honeycombed layers. In the ballroom he stopped his tour for a moment to watch the party. Suddenly he dashed out onto the floor between the dancers, leaned down and scraped off a bit of wax with his fingernail. "Someone might have slipped on it," he explained to the friend with him. "But why do it yourself?" the friend reproached him. "You've a hundred people to do such things." "But I was here," he said.

One of (the reporters) caught Statler resting with his arm thrown over the arm of a low-backed chair. Without being prompted, Statler remarked to him, "I had a battle to get this chair made with a low back. The artist said the back ought to be higher and have a knob on it, but I said: 'Make it low and comfortable so a man can hook his arm over the corner.' I told him that if it was comfortable it would be artistic."

A *Detroit News* columnist, who by-lined himself The Grouch, wrote:

Well (said the Grouch) the newspaper men of Detroit and other cities pried open the new Hotel Statler all right and garner it from us it was some premiere and we not only opened it we closed it and all in one night and I went home and the missus said did you have a good time did I I said I should kiss a lamb that I did I suppose it's a grand hotel she said grand isn't a bit too strong I said it's magnificent I can't remember when I have been in a hotel she said we couldn't afford to live at half as nice as the Statler is I said did you meet Mr. Statler she said yes I said and I and he will never regret that we built that hotel and got Mr. Bergman here from Ottawa to manage it were there many speeches she said yes I said and a filibuster conducted by a man from a Chicago hotel paper I said that's what made me late how she said why I said the posse that had to work over the English language after he got through with it to bring it to and did Mr. Statler talk she said yes I said and entertainingly too and she said what did he say and I said he said whatter we here for boys why she said what did he mean by that search me I said but a young fellow there seemed to know who was he she said I dunno I said he was a perfect stranger to me and she said what did he do oh I said he kept coming over to our table and pouring things in a glass I guess he's a friend of Mr. Statler's I said and he certainly is a very handy man to have around a dining room but I had to give up I said I couldn't even catch up with him.

CHAPTER 18

AMERICAN HOTEL ASSOCIATION

In the year 1910 Mark Twain died, and so did Mary Baker Eddy; Jack Johnson licked James J. Jeffries for the world heavyweight boxing championship; Marie Dressler played to standing room in "Tillie's Nightmare"; prohibition began inching its way across the nation as the State of Tennessee went dry; the president of Princeton University, Woodrow Wilson, won his first public office and became Governor of New Jersey.

In 1910 Ellsworth Statler dipped his big toe in hotel politics. Soon he was up to his waist, and then almost over his head.

With the advent of the automobile and the resultant boom in hotel construction, there were a number of industrywide problems that forced hotel men to band together in trade associations. Once together, somebody had to take charge, and since Statler had a congenital inability to be a follower, he fought for leadership. The fact that his principal opponent was a man who wore nose glasses attached to a black ribbon and carried chamois gloves and a cane — well, Statler's very viscera were in opposition.

On January 31 there gathered at Chicago's Palmer House sixty prominent hotelkeepers of the Middle and Far West. What had brought them together was the rising incident of crime in their hotels, especially the passing of bad checks. They formed the American Hotel Protective Association and appointed a committee to interview private detective agencies about possible solutions to their problems. Statler was not an officer of the Association nor a member of the committee.

The Association met again in August to adopt a permanent constitution and by-laws, and to elect the following officers:

President: Sam F. Dutton, the Albany, Denver.

First vice-president: Henry W. Lawrence, the Claypool, Indianapolis.

Second vice-president: F. J. Taggart, Hotel Loyal, Omaha.

Third vice-president: Kirk Harris, the Grand, San Francisco.

Secretary and Treasurer: John K. Blatchford, Auditorium Tower, Chicago.

Executive Committee: Chas. C. Horton, the Metropole, Chicago, for three years, chairman.

Fred Van Orman, St. George Hotel, Evansville, two years.

H. Stanley Green, Plankinton House, Milwaukee, two years.

Rome Miller, Hotel Rome, Omaha, one year.

E. M. Tierney, Hotel Marlborough, New York, one year.

Protective board: W. C. Vierbucken, Palmer House, Chicago, chairman.

John C. Roth, Great Northern Hotel, Chicago.

Charles McHugh, Lexington Hotel, Chicago.

Max L. Teich, The Kaiserhof, Chicago.

Alex Dryburgh, The Southern, Chicago.

Statler was not even nominated for any of the offices. Which did not mean, however, that the Association didn't hear from him. He had done a lot of homework since their last meeting and he presented to his colleagues a detailed plan for protection against bad checks. The September issue of *The Hotel Monthly* gave a detailed report:

E. M. STATLER

At the meeting in Chicago August 23 to form the American Hotel Protective Association, E. M. Statler of Hotel Statler, Buffalo, presented a plan for hotelkeepers' protection possessing so many novel ideas that, after discussion, it was placed in the hands of a committee to consider and report on at the next annual meeting of the protective association.

Mr. Statler's proposition in brief is: All paper cashed by a hotel to have stamps affixed at the cost of the person asking the accommodation; the sale of stamps to produce a revenue sufficient for all purposes of capturing and punishing criminals who prey upon hotels, and to reimburse hotelkeepers for the money lost by them on bad paper. He would have the hotels carry these stamps in quantities and denominations sufficient for all their needs, and suggested a ten cent stamp be affixed to all pieces of paper under $25; a 20-cent stamp on paper under $50; a 40-cent stamp for under $100; and limiting the amount of the association's liability to $150 on any single piece of paper. He would make it imperative to put a stamp on all paper, no matter whether the person asking the accommodation be an old and valued patron or a friend. There should be no exception.

Mr. Statler gave statistics based on the amount of paper cashed by his hotel and other hotels, to show that a very large sum can be raised for protection in this way, estimated to exceed half a million dollars annually. "When my plan is working," said Mr. Statler, "the hotelkeeper will not have to worry about any paper he may have cashed. He deposits it in the bank, and that is the end of it so far as he is concerned. The bank returns any and all bad paper to the guarantee headquarters, where machinery to punish the passers of bad paper is put into operation."

He would have a system of reports warning hotels against criminals and holding hotelkeepers to the same care in the cashing of paper they exercise now, and where lack of care is shown, for the hotelkeeper to stand his loss.

Mr. Statler's paper was debated and thrashed over for about two hours. Mr. Wooley of the Ponchartrain Hotel,

124

Detroit, found the most objections to it. He said, "You tax honest men to pay for the work of criminals. One stamp that insures refunding of the loss on a piece of bad paper is made good by 99 stamps on good paper that should not be taxed.

"Paper, on which the party asking accommodation has already paid a premium in the way of exchange, is, by your stamp proposition, made to pay a double tax.

"Business is done largely thru the medium of paper. There is very little cash in circulation. Mr. Statler's plan, therefore, would injure, rather than help.

"What about the restaurant customers who pay by check?

"What about boarders who pay by check?

"What about banquets, conventions, and such like, when the money is received by check? Are all of these to be considered? Where do you draw the line?

"What about subterfuges that may be resorted to in cashing bad paper for the patron who refuses to pay the stamp tax and would go 'to the other hotel' rather than do so, as, for instance, his getting his check cashed at a cigar stand?

"Our losses," said Mr. Wooley, "on bad paper average only one mill, and we would rather stand that than impose it on the public."

Mr. Swearingen of the St. Anthony, San Antonio, said, "I would not become a member if I was obliged to make the guest pay for this accommodation."

It became obvious that Statler's idea was not a good one, but at least it was an idea. The hostility to it was out of proportion to its faults, because many hotel men simply did not like Statler. They were jealous of him, to begin with, and the service innovations he was forcing them to adopt was costing them a lot of money. Nor did Statler do anything to win their friendship. His bluntness, his lack of polish and indifference to dress, his impatience with "Fancy Dans" was all calculated to set him apart from his colleagues who were trying to improve their public image.

E. M. STATLER

When the regional American Hotel Protective Association expanded to become a truly national trade association and in 1917 became the American Hotel Association, the first president was not the rough-hewn Statler, but his opposite, elegant Frank Dudley.

Dudley not only wore custom-tailored suits and chamois gloves and beribboned spectacles and carried a cane; he not only looked like the Prime Minister of Ruritania, but he acted the part. To him the hotel business was romantic, a continuous operetta. He was the president of the United Hotels Company which was in the process of rapid expansion, and here again he was the opposite of Statler. Not for him was the long and agonizing research of a town's business potential; he seemed to choose hotel sites by intuition, for pure drama. Dudley was having a love affair with the hotel business; Statler conducted a marriage.

"Dudley is going to lead the AHA into trouble," Statler growled to a friend. He was right.

The project which brought financial trouble to the AHA was a perfectly sound and even necessary one: the attempt to supply trained hotel management personnel by education on the college level. Dudley was especially aware of this problem, as was one of his friends, J. Leslie Kincaid, chairman of the board of the American Hotels Corporation. These two had divided their areas of activity; Dudley's United Hotels was to concentrate on big hotels in the cities, while Kincaid's firm would construct in the smaller communities.

As their hotels proliferated they became painfully aware of the shortage of trained managers and assistant managers and even department heads such as chefs.

For many years Europe had been the reservoir of skilled hotel men and hardly a major hotel (except Statler's) opened in America without the proud announcement of the fact that the managing director or the maitre d' or the chef had come from Switzerland or France. The demand had outrun the supply. Moreover, the Americans were generally building a different kind of hotel. These were neither intimate inns nor luxury establishments in the grand tradition; they were commercial and family hotels. Most of Europe's hotel men neither understood nor wanted to understand this kind of operation.

Faced with this, AHA's president Dudley did a logical thing: he appointed an education committee to look into the problem and come up with recommendations. As chairman of the committee he named Waldorf Astoria's Lucius Boomer. Ellsworth Statler's reaction was predictable: when a man who wore yellow gloves appointed a New Yorker. . . well, something slippery was likely to result.

The committee obtained the aid of the Federal Board of Vocational Training in the study and L. S. Hawkins' final report recommended: 1. An intensive educational-research program; 2. The establishment of a school of hotel management at Cornell University; 3. Cash grants to high schools and trade schools for vocational training, particularly in the area of cooks and bakers. The program called for an investment of $2,000,000.

Enthusiasm in the AHA ran high.

About this time there was an obscure young man named Howard Meek who wrote trade journal articles deploring the fact that while there were college courses in journalism and banking and even in agriculture, there were none in hotel management. Upon investigation the AHA learned that Meek taught a course on resort management in Boston University and he seemed a likely man to head up the proposed school at Cornell.

The first meeting between Meek and Statler was not a happy one. They were much the same size, short and slight of build, but where Statler's face was square and aggressive, Meek's face seemed much as his name. Surely that tough and grizzled infighter Statler would chew up the mild young man. Not at all!

"How you gonna teach hotel work in school?" Statler growled. "What do you know about it, anyway?"

"I didn't claim to know so darned much," Meek snapped back. "But I've had some practical experience, if that's what you mean. I've worked the resort hotels in the mountains."

"Humph!" Statler said and turned away.

The AHA's great enthusiasm for the new research-educational program was not sufficient to produce the two-million-dollar fund originally projected. The more modest figure of $750,000 was set, and of this only $150,000 was pledged by the members, and only $21,000 paid in. The hotel men were reluctant to put their money where their mouths were.

Nevertheless, in 1922 the AHA administration signed a contract with Cornell for the establishment of a hotel school under the direction of Howard Meek, and promised $20,000 a year for the school, $70,000 a year for research. Then the AHA had to borrow the money to meet the first year's obligation.

Fearing financial difficulties ahead, Meek didn't spend the promised $90,000 a year, but reduced it to $57,000. Even so, the AHA was unable to keep up its payments to the university. Little more than one year later the Association was $100,000 in debt, and with every prospect of going deeper.

If there was a cardinal sin in Statler's book it was "owed money." He declared war upon the Association's debt and upon the man primarily responsible for incurring it, Frank Dudley. He challenged the right of the leadership to incur debts without a plan for paying them off. "For our trade association to have unpaid bills is to besmirch the entire industry," he declared in a ringing statement of principles.

Not only did Statler contribute some rather high-flown rhetoric but something else of even greater importance — money. He offered personally to underwrite $70,000 of the Association's indebtedness, if the other members would pay off the remaining $30,000. Their pride stung, the hotel men could do little but follow Statler's lead.

In 1925 the AHA convened in Colorado Springs and Mr. Frank Dudley stepped down. Elected in his place was Statler's man, Thomas D. Green. It took Statler fifteen years to gain control of the hotel trade association; if it had required twice the time, his zest for battle would have been undiminished.

When he at last assumed power he was not, however, the same man who had first entered the lists. By 1925 Statler had learned that the man in yellow gloves and the New York slickers were right in a number of things.

CHAPTER 19

THE ST. LOUIS STATLER

Fighting for control of the American Hotel Association did not mean that Statler neglected his own company. With three hotels operating successfully, he decided upon further expansion. He did not rush into an orgy of building, as did Frank Dudley's United Hotels, but carefully researched the towns that were competing for his attention. He held firmly to his creed that the three rules for a success hotel were "Location, location, location."

Sentiment played a role, to be sure. When St. Louis asked him to build a hotel there, he remembered the town's generosity to him after his accident at the Inside Inn, and he gave them a hotel. His decision was announced in *Salesmanship*, the house organ:

IT'S AT ST. LOUIS

Everybody in the organization probably knows by this time that the next Hotel Statler is to be at St. Louis. Thus are half a dozen contradictory rumors set at rest.

Plans are not yet complete in all details, but it is certain that the new house will resemble those at Cleveland and Detroit. The location is at Washington, Ninth and St. Charles Streets, on a site 150 by 130 feet.

Mr. Statler made a flying trip ... early this month to conclude the deal with Mr. Tom W. Bennett, president of the Mortgage Trust Company, St. Louis, and his associates. He was met in St. Louis on April 6th by Mr. Mosier and Mr. Hinkley, and negotiations moved smoothly to a successful conclusion.

It is not too early to begin boosting St. Louis. And you can paste it in your hat that it's going to be a hotel we'll all be proud of. And by the way: are you going to be ready to graduate into a bigger job by the time St. Louis has some bigger jobs for salesmen to fill?

The use of the word "salesman" was not an inadvertence. Statler was campaigning to make his entire staff, from manager down to bus boy, alert to the fact that every contact with a guest gave them an opportunity to *sell* Statler service and courtesy.

As construction got under way in St. Louis, Statler discovered he had no good advance man, someone to introduce him to the town's social leaders, as Homer Warren had done in Detroit. He had close ties with the business leaders, but not with society, not with the people who could make it chic to dine at the hotel. With the absence of such a local champion, he had no choice but to send in a stranger. He gave this job to a member of his staff, James H. McCabe.

"Jimmy," he said, "you have a nice, affable personality and you make friends readily. I'm sending you to St. Louis. I'll put you up at the Missouri Athletic Club, and I want you to meet people, and attend all the functions and parties, and make friends for us so that when the hotel opens we'll have a backlog of people who will patronize us. I'm sending David Lauber out as general manager. David is a fine gentleman, but he's not the greeter type. You are. Go out there and do a job for us."

McCabe did a fine job of public relations and by the time the twenty-story structure was finished, the entire town was full of eager anticipation. The day before the opening ceremonies, on November 4, 1917, a unique editorial appeared in the St. Louis *Post-Dispatch*:

The Statler Hotel, which was formally opened yesterday, puts St. Louis on the modern hotel map.

E. M. STATLER

That the Statler Hotel Company chose St. Louis as the fourth city in its group of hotels and built here so costly and beautiful a structure, with a complete plant and rich equipment that equals those of the best metropolitan hotels, is significant of the confidence of the ability of St. Louis to support a hotel of this type now and of faith in the city's future.

The building and equipment are not intended to provide for the traveling public alone; a large part of the space and the best of the equipment are provided for the use of St. Louisans. Travelers would be satisfied with comfortable rooms at reasonable prices and an adequate restaurant for their simple requirements, but the Statler has a half dozen dining rooms, from the grill in the basement to the superb ball and banquet room on the 19th floor.

The success of this, as of all hotels in cities of the St. Louis class, depends as much upon St. Louis as upon the traveling public. If St. Louisans do not appreciate and use its special equipment it will be at least a partial failure — it will be a mere tavern for the passing traveler. If St. Louisans prove their appreciation of the best that is offered, the Statler Hotel is only a station in the path of progress for the greater St. Louis to come.

We feel sure we express the hearty sentiment of all St. Louis in welcoming the Statler forces to St. Louis and congratulating them upon the splendid result they have achieved.

Statler had succeeded in endowing his two-and-one-half-million-dollar hotel with the aura of a civic project, made the entire town feel responsible for its welfare. This was a remarkable business achievement.

There was one aspect of the new hotel that caused comment in the trade press — it was pretty much a carbon copy of the previous Statler houses. Henry J. Bohn, in *Hotel World*, wrote:

If I were compelled to describe the new Hotel Statler of St. Louis in five words I would write: *It is a Statler*

THE ST. LOUIS STATLER

Hotel. Any man who has seen the Statler Hotels of Buffalo, Cleveland and Detroit, and particularly in the latter two cities, will recognize a Statler Hotel as far as he can see one, and entering it he knows instantly that he is in one of the Statler public palaces.

This means that Statler has created a *type.* All he tries to do in adding another link to his chain, another numeral to the Statler list, is to improve in detail where experience has proven some change will add to appearance or utility, or will add to the convenience of or please patrons. Statler is the father of *hotel standardization* in America, and that means in the world. This is saying a very big thing. When a man builds a hotel and operates it for several years, builds another, and then another, and another, and the last one is on the same general lines as the others except as to minor details, we know he has *"struck it."* ...

When you see the new St. Louis Statler, you see the Detroit and Cleveland Statlers with the latest touches in Statler architecture, equipment, furnishings and art.

There were sound business reasons for this sameness. Not only did mass purchasing save money, but equipment and supplies were interchangeable. Firm inventory control was made easier by the fact that silver, dishes, glassware and even furnishings could be shipped from one hotel to another. Louis Rorimer had managed to decorate guestrooms with variety but always with related colors so that draperies and spreads and rugs could be interchanged.

Statler's construction innovations were based upon efficient usage and privacy. The salesmen's sample rooms where they could display goods were always on the top floor, isolated from the regular guests. The ballroom and private dining rooms were on the floor above the lobby to give people attending these functions privacy from the traffic on the main floor. The ballroom usually had a separate entrance and separate elevators placed apart from the regular ones.

There was a unique kitchen arrangement. Most hotel builders placed their kitchens in the basement where space was considered less valuable, but Statler put his on the first floor where there would be greater efficiency. He made his kitchen three-sided and built the eating rooms around it, thus making one facility serve the dining room, a coffee shop and a cafe.

Very occasionally a guest would complain, "When you've seen one Statler Hotel you've seen them all."

To this Statler would reply, "If they are the best, there is nothing wrong with standardization."

CHAPTER 20

"LIFE IS SERVICE"

The one thing Statler could not standardize, or even make logical, was his personal response to money. Throughout his life he fluctuated between extravagance and tightfistedness.

On the occasion of his fiftieth birthday he threw an elaborate party for his relatives, about twenty of them, and gave each $10,000. On the following morning he stopped by the concession cigar counter in the lobby of his Buffalo hotel to buy his daily candy bar. He tossed his money down and started away when the sales girl called after him.

"Mr. Statler, that candy has been increased in price two pennies."

"Two pennies!" Statler repeated darkly. He studied the bar in his hand for a moment and then tossed it on the counter. "Give me my money back. It's not worth it."

Statler hotels were the first to offer laundry service to the guests and the boss quite naturally took advantage of it. He sent a suit of underwear down to the laundry for mending and when it was returned there was a note from the head housekeeper pinned to it: "Dear Mr. Statler, The seamstresses find it most difficult to do a satisfactory job on this garment. We have mended it so often that there is little of the original fabric left. We are now mending the mends. I just wanted to let you know that we are doing the best we can under these conditions."

He wore cheap, ready-made suits and a hat so battered as to cause the other hotel men to take action. He was invited to a small dinner given by Tom Green of the American Hotel Association, George W. Sweeney of the Commodore Hotel, and Elmore Green, president of the New York State Hotel Association.

"Mr. Statler," said Tom Green, acting as toastmaster, "we have summoned you to teach you. The shapeless and shameless chapeau you wear is a reflection upon us all because it stands as the symbol of poverty. Therefore, we have taken steps to make you look like what you are — the greatest hotel man in the business."

Thereupon Statler was presented with a silk topper, a derby, a pearl grey homburg, a Bangkok straw and a panama. Statler grinned and thanked his hosts and promised to make good use of the gifts. Some weeks later George Sweeney saw the hatter from whom they had purchased the headgear.

"George," the hatter said, "Statler's outwitted you. All those hats were sent back to my store with a note which read, 'Take back all this junk, give me book credit, and send me a decent $3 hat once a year for a hundred years.'"

Even when his own health was involved Statler found it difficult to decide what to spend. Because of the burns and the grafts on his legs he had periodic difficulty with varicose veins. One day he said to Frank McKowne, his secretary and later first vice president of the company, "My legs are hurting me, Mac. Doc Boswell says that the Mayo Brothers can fix me up. Write them and find out what they'll charge."

It was not easy to get an advance quotation for surgery from the distinguished Mayo Brothers, but McKowne kept after them until they finally said it would cost fifteen hundred dollars, more or less. When McKowne reported this, Statler cried, "Fifteen hundred dollars! I won't pay it! My legs hurt, but not that much."

He never had the operation.

One winter day he returned to Buffalo after a short

trip to Florida and had lunch with McKowne when he announced casually, "I bought a boat and she's a beauty. Named the *Miramar*. Cost five hundred thousand when she was new but I got her from an estate for two hundred and fifty thousand."

"Did you pay for her?" McKowne asked.

"Sure."

"How?"

"I wrote a check on the Guaranty Bank."

"You don't have over ten thousand in that account at the moment."

"That's your problem," Statler snapped, and changed the subject.

Statler slipped away from his office for a half-hour one afternoon and returned wearing a pair of eyeglasses. He was very pleased with them, said they helped his vision considerably. He had purchased them at a nearby Woolworth's ten-cent store.

There was some irony in the fact that Statler was growing rich in an industry that paid notoriously poor wages. He determined to do something about this. Much of his labor force (bellmen, maids, waitresses, porters, bus boys, etc.) was unskilled and traditionally transient. These men and women were given little respect by their superiors and therefore had little for themselves. They could feel no sense of accomplishment on the job because it was one that anybody could perform. Their source of gratification was almost entirely from the money they earned.

Statler attacked this problem on two fronts. He began a psychological campaign to give every employee dignity and pride of job, and he established a program of profit sharing. These steps were taken for hardheaded business reasons, for he was convinced that only prideful and secure employees could give the guests the kind of courtesy and efficiency he demanded.

Just as Statler had been the pioneer in hotel construction, now he became the pioneer in management-employee relations. He was first to give hotel men and women a six-day week, vacations with pay, and free health service. In 1916 the *Hotel Gazette* commented on this radical policy:

> We commend Mr. Statler. He has done a thing for hoteldom that will be far-reaching in its beneficial effects. A long forward step has been taken.

A "matching savings" plan was announced by Statler. He promised to match dollar for dollar all deposits the employee made in the company savings account. Statler set aside large blocks of common stock for his profit sharing plan. The employees could purchase this 7 percent stock at $100 a share on installment payments. The payments were deducted from wages, the employee receiving 7 percent interest on the money deducted until the stock was paid for. With every $250 worth of preferred stock purchased, the employee received free one share of common stock.

There were those who did not approve of these programs. Hotel owners, who had to compete with Statler for labor, feared that he was setting precedents that would drive up their own labor costs; they feared also that the better workers would gravitate to Statler. They were right on both counts.

Even within Statler's organization there were some misgivings among the workers. A few skeptics said that the savings plan was a trick to find out how much a man could save, and then his regular wages would be cut by that amount. Some of the older employees objected to the free medical service because they thought it a trick to discover a man's physical weaknesses to be used as an excuse for firing him.

Some of the critics simply thought that the program

would not achieve the ends for which it was created. *Hotel World* wrote:

> Will the employees of the great Hotels Statler Company ... appreciate this remarkable innovation? Will it make them more faithful, loyal, industrious?

Statler's answer was brief: "Members of a firm are always more interested in their jobs."

Despite the misgivings and suspicions that popped up here and there, the overwhelming majority of the employees joined one or more of the various plans, and because of that were able eventually to retire in security.

Because of all this did they give better service to the public? Indeed they did, and not entirely because of the money. Having presented the carrot, from time to time Statler gave them the stick.

The generally low level of hotel service during this period was revealed in a letter written by a traveler named Dr. Frank Crane. The letter was to a chain (not Statler's) but found its way into the trade press. It read:

> People in hotels want a cordial welcome, a kindly atmosphere and human warmth of feeling which you do not give them. I found two things in your inns, obsequiousness and indifference. The porter was very anxious to carry my little valise that weighed about ten pounds. The cloak room girl insisted on checking my hat and cane which I could easily take care of myself. The waiters manifested a lively interest in my wellbeing only at the crucial moment when I was counting my change. Venality and subservience stuck out all over these persons. Their acts and manner dumbly shrieked, "How much is this fellow going to give us?" The impression I got was not that I was there to be made comfortable, but was there to be fleeced. I was not a guest, I was prey.

The letter supplied Statler with a perfect springboard from which to launch his own philosophy of hotel keeping and of life:

E. M. STATLER

"Life is service. The one who progresses is the one who gives his fellow human beings a little more, a little better service."

When he talked about service he meant that it should be given to *all*, without reservation. He spelled it out for his employees in a special bulletin:

A man may wear a red necktie, a green vest and tan shoes, and still be a gentleman. The unpretentious man with the soft voice may possess the wealth of Croesus. The stranger in cowhide boots, broadbrim and rusty black, may be president of a railroad or a senator from over the ridge. You cannot afford to be superior or sullen with any patron of this hotel.

Out of this philosophy there evolved the formal "Statler Service Code." Every employee received a copy and was required not only to memorize it but to keep a copy of it on his person during all working hours. The Code read:

It is the business of a good hotel to cater to the public. It is the avowed business of the Hotel Statler to please the public better than any other hotel in the world.

Have everyone feel that for his money we want to give him more sincere service than he ever before received at any hotel.

Never be perky, pungent, or fresh. The guests pays your salary as well as mine. He is your immediate benefactor.

Hotel service, that is Hotel Statler service, means the limit of courteous, efficient attention from each particular employee to each particular guest. It is the object of the Hotel Statler to sell its guest the best service in the world.

No employee of this hotel is allowed the privilege of arguing any point with a guest. He must adjust the matter at once to the guest's satisfaction or call his superior to adjust it. Wrangling has no place in Hotel Statler.

In all minor discussions between Statler employees and Statler guests the employee is dead wrong, from the guest's point of view and from ours.

"LIFE IS SERVICE"

Any Statler employee who is wise and discreet enough to merit tips is wise and discreet enough to render a like service whether he is tipped or not.

Any Statler employee who fails to give service or who fails to thank the guest who gives him something, falls short of Statler standards.

As the number of employees grew into the hundreds, Statler faced an increasing problem of communication with them. He wanted them to identify with the organization, to understand and *believe* that whatever was good for the hotel was good for them. Much as he would have liked to, it was physically impossible for him to give a personal pep talk to every employee every week. He did the next best thing, he established a monthly house organ so that he might talk to his people in print.

Statler Salesmanship was the title of the publication and it was printed on heavy coated stock and measured 3½" x 8". The odd size was designed so that employees might conveniently carry it in their pockets. A printing plant was installed in the basement of the Buffalo Statler and 12,000 copies were struck off each month. On the first page of each issue Statler wrote a rather hortatory essay on some aspect of life and work. Typical was the article in the April 1914 issue:

The hotel employee who has the habit of saving money is on the road to success, however small his salary and his savings. The saving habit marks him as a man who will make good... If a man saves regularly... he is accumulating more than money: He is building his own independence. He is building self-reliance, and character and opportunity. He is putting himself where fear of losing his job, and worry about money can't touch him. He is worth more to his employer, because he can do better work. He is worth more to himself, because he is freer, happier... The man who can't save anything out of a small salary is just as unable to save out of a large one... Get the habit!

141

Pages two and three were devoted to more concrete aspects of the job of hotel salesmanship. The remainder of the 16 pages carried news of the employees, both their business and private lives. The over-all purpose of the publication was to supply the "glue" to hold the "Statler family" together.

The publication drew far more attention than Statler had anticipated. First off, it was unique in the hotel industry and seemed destined to be copied by other hotel men who found it difficult (for whatever reason) to communicate with their employees. Its fame spread beyond the industry, with business and political leaders asking to be put on the mailing list. Using plain words and common sense, Statler's thesis (what was good for management was good for labor) found wide acceptance.

For all the public success of *Salesmanship*, Statler could not be certain that every one of his employees read it. He fretted about this for a time, then came up with a solution; he introduced a new weekly publication entitled "Bulletin for Department Meetings." Right below the title were the words, "To be read by every Department Head at meeting with employees during week of . . . . . ."

Any department head who failed to call his people together and read the Bulletin would not be a department head for long.

In the Bulletin, Statler was more informal, more chatty than in *Salesmanship*. He employed parables and fables to make his points. One of the issues carried the "Story of the Three Stone Cutters."

Here is a simple story — so simple you may miss the point. Therefore, listen carefully. Here it is:

Three stone cutters were driving their chisels into a massive block of Vermont granite. A stranger who happened along asked the first cutter what he was doing.

"I'm cutting stone," growled the laborer.

"And you?" he asked the second.

"I'm working for $7.50 a day," he replied.

When the question was put to the third, his face lit up and he answered, "I'm building a cathedral."

We're one of those three kinds of stone cutters. I hope each one of you can say, "I'm building a cathedral."

Many of the Bulletins carried disciplinary threats. In one issue Statler told the "Story of the Ox and the Mule."

Down in Virginia a farmer had an ox and a mule that he hitched together to a plow. One night, after several days of continuous plowing, and after the ox and mule had been stabled and provendered for the night, the ox said to the mule: "We've been working pretty hard, let's play off sick tomorrow and lie here in the stalls all day."

"You can if you want to," returned the mule, "but I believe I'll go to work."

So the next morning when the farmer came out the ox played off sick. The farmer bedded him down with clean straw, gave him fresh hay, a bucket of oats and bran mixed, left him for the day and went forth with the mule to plow.

All that day the ox lay in his stall, chewed his cud and nodded, slowly blinked his eyes, and gently swished his tail.

That night when the mule came in, the ox asked him how they got along plowing alone all day. "Well," said the mule, "it was hard and we didn't get much done and —"

"Did the old man have anything to say about me?" interrupted the ox.

"No," replied the mule.

"Well, then" went on the ox, "I believe I'll play off again tomorrow; it was certainly fine laying here all day and resting."

"That's up to you," said the mule, "but I'll go out and plow."

So the next day the ox played off again, was bedded down with clean straw, provendered with hay, bran and oats, and lay all day nodding, blinking, chewing his cud and gently swishing his tail.

When the mule came in at night the ox asked him again how they had gotten along without him.

"About the same as yesterday," replied the mule coldly.

"Did the old man have anything to say to you about me?" again inquired the ox.

"No," replied the mule, "not to me, but he did have a damn long talk with the butcher on the way home."

CHAPTER 21

BUILDING A MANAGEMENT TEAM

As his empire grew Statler learned that it was easier to find a good worker than a good boss. The hiring and disciplining of 5,000 cooks, maids, bellboys and porters was not nearly so difficult as hiring four corporate management men. He was demanding, certainly, but there were just not many trained executives available in this young industry.

Speaking to an AHA convention, he said, ". . . I found that I must buy more experience, or grow it. And the market (had) . . . mighty little experience to offer."

So he began to "grow" his own men. Of the six who ultimately moved to power (and wealth) under Statler, only one had any hotel or related experience. Of the others, two were newspapermen and two were lawyers. Whatever their backgrounds or previous experience, these men had to learn a new way of working — the Statler way. What was involved here was an attitude, a cast of mind. He could, and did, teach them the techniques of hotel management, but what they had to contribute to the process was a complete personal commitment. Over the years there were a number of casualties among the men who thought that twelve hours a day six days a week was sufficient labor. There were casualties among the men who resented the demands made upon them but attempted to conceal the resentment. What was required of them could not be simulated, not before Statler's cool, measuring eyes.

If a man did not find the hotel business absolutely fascinating, completely rewarding, if he was not a true believer and ready to make almost any personal sacrifice for that belief, he had no future with Statler.

At the time of the Cleveland construction in 1912 Statler put together his first corporate staff. He took the title of President; the office of Secretary-Treasurer went to Frank Hinkley, ex-newspaperman and for a time manager of the Buffalo hotel; Charles Mosier became First Vice President; and completing the staff was W. J. (Statler's brother) who for a time held the title of Second Vice President.

There followed several years of the most trying times for all these men as they tried to learn how to work together. There was waste motion, confusion and misunderstandings on all sides, and it was primarily Statler's fault. He established no clear-cut areas of responsibility, no lines of authority; he made all decisions himself and then seemed surprised at the lack of initiative in his staff. Most demoralizing of all, he not infrequently gave two men the same assignment, "just to see who'd do it best."

What finally saved the management from flying apart was the fact that Statler could learn. All his life he found it difficult to delegate authority, but he knew that he should and he worked at overcoming this fault. Moreover, as the size of his organization increased it became impossible for him to be everywhere, to make every decision, much as he might want to. Between 1913 and 1917 he built a new staff, hiring men he respected and to whom, he promised himself, he would eventually give major authority and responsibility.

Four men finally came to the top in this yeasty organization: Frank A. McKowne, C. B. Stoner, David Newton and John L. Hennessy.

McKowne was the first one of the "Big Four" to be hired. In the autumn of 1913 Statler remarked to an old Buffalo friend, William Summers, that he was looking for an executive secretary, a man who would work 24 hours a day.

"I think I have the man for you," the Judge said. "I'll send him around if he's interested."

The following day young Frank McKowne presented himself to Statler in the crowded office on the top floor of the Buffalo hotel. He was a short man, no taller than Statler, and he had finely chiseled features which he could keep under control no matter the provocation.

"Well, what do you have to say for yourself?" Statler barked at him.

After a moment of careful thought, McKowne said, "I don't drink or smoke."

"I don't hold that either against you or for you," Statler said.

After another moment of thought, McKowne said, "I'm a lawyer. I received my degree this last spring."

"I don't hold that against you, either," Statler said, but this time he grinned.

McKowne was hired and it did not take many weeks for Statler to realize that he had chosen the right man. Statler worked with broad visions and grand plans; he was impatient with the implementing details. McKowne, on the other hand, was an excellent detail man. Statler set policy, McKowne saw that the policy was carried out. He saw to it that the bolts were in the right holes, the gears were properly lubricated. And he was tireless. He could work around the clock without the slightest resentment or loss of interest.

Statler was given to middle-of-the-night inspirations and since he could not have an idea without acting upon it, he would immediately call a conference. McKowne became accustomed to these summonses and would climb out of bed, dress, and drive to Soldiers Place where he'd work with the boss till dawn. It was not until the first week of August, 1925, that he made any objection.

147

On that day he had brought his wife and new daughter home from the hospital. When the phone rang at three in the morning he dashed to lift the receiver and silence the bell, for he was certain that to wake a sleeping baby would damage its health.

"I just got a new idea on mattress quality control," came Statler's high, wide-awake voice. "Come on over and we'll talk about it."

"It's four o'clock in the morning and we just got the baby home from the hospital and this is ridiculous," McKowne exploded.

"Oh," Statler said, and hung up.

The next day McKowne received a letter from the boss. It was an apology . . . sort of. It read:

> I do not know whether you know it has been the custom — whenever there is a new baby in the organization — to start a bank account for that baby — and it is with sincere pleasure I send the enclosed check for the little girl.

Over the years Statler came to depend more and more on McKowne for routine management. He became Executive Vice President of the organization and then (upon Statler's death) President.

Two years after hiring McKowne, Statler said to him, "I think we need a financial man, a controller." McKowne nodded agreement. Statler continued, "We're getting too big for the haphazard way of handling money. We need a watchdog, a man who loves figures just for their own sake. And we need the best. I'll write a letter to Harvard."

"The Dean of the Business School," McKowne suggested.

"Hell, no! I'll write the President."

Through the correspondence with Harvard, Statler found just the kind of man he had hoped for. His name was C. B. Stoner; he had graduated from Harvard, been a statistician for the university's Bureau of Business Research, and was currently a Professor of Business Administration at Carnegie Institute of Technology. He was not particularly eager to leave Carnegie Tech and come to Buffalo, which made him doubly attractive in Statler's eyes.

In the end Stoner could not resist Statler's wooing and he came into the organization with the title of General Auditor. He entered quietly into the organization for it was his nature to be without jollity or aggression. He was a square, solid man whose face seemed forever in repose. It was inevitable that he and Statler would clash, for he represented the cold and hard business realities that Statler often wished to ignore.

"By hell's fire, I don't want you coming in here and telling me what I can and can't do!" Statler flared at him one day.

"It is not I who tells you what you can or can't do," Stoner replied quietly with no change of expression. "I merely present the figures. *They* are the ones that tell you."

Statler snorted and walked away. Later in the day he growled to McKowne, "That Stoner has sure got the right name."

One of the most glaring inefficiencies Stoner found was the lack of uniform auditing systems for all the hotels. Centralized cost control was all but impossible under these conditions and Stoner drew up a plan to correct this. The plan called for an expansion of his own department and the installation of some costly auditing equipment. He put his recommendations on paper, presented them to Statler and seated himself across the desk to answer any questions.

After carefully reading the paper, Statler tossed it on his desk and gave an inscrutable look at his General Auditor. Finally he spoke, not with questions but with a story.

"Several months ago I ran into Henry Ford at our Detroit house and we had a chat. You might be interested in what he had to say."

149

A barely perceptible nod came from Stoner.

"Ford told me that his people were forever after him to put in a modern statistical department and finally he gave in. Some months later he was strolling through the plant and came upon a vast room lined with filing cases and full of complicated tabulating machines. A dozen people were opening and closing files and operating the machines. He went up to one of them and said, 'What do you do here?'

"'We prepare statistics,' was the reply.

"'What do you do with the statistics?' Ford asked.

"'We file them.'

"'Oh,' said Ford.

"Upon leaving the department Ford came upon a production engineer. 'Didn't you tell me that you needed more space?' he demanded. 'Well, you can have that room in there.'

"And the interesting thing about all this, Stoner, is that I don't believe that Ford has sold one less auomobile for not having that department."

The conference was obviously at an end, so Stoner stood up, nodded, and left. This implied threat did not intimidate him and he continued to send memoranda to his employer. What he was trying to do was install a system that would bring down cost per unit, per rented room, and in the end the logic was so overwhelming that Statler gave in to him. The cost accounting methods that Stoner created for the Statler chain eventually became standard for the industry.

This quiet, precise man became a balance wheel in the organization which was top-heavy with dreams and enthusiasms. All new projects were submitted to him for financial analysis, and whenever his advice was "no," Statler would strike his fist against his desk and cry, "Hell's delight! I'm tempted to throw out your whole damn department and give my auditing to Ernst & Ernst!"

He never did. Instead, he gave Stoner a whopping big bonus of Statler stock and made him Treasurer.

The seventeen-year boom in hotel construction which started at the turn of the 20th Century and lasted until America entered World War I, resulted in increasingly severe competition. Statler had the jump in this "race for the guest," but as other hotel men copied his construction and management ideas, his competitive edge began to shrink. He counterattacked with his unique idea of service, with his philosophy "the guest is always right." To spread this he launched an advertising campaign of dimensions never before seen in the hotel industry.

The advertising agency which helped him create and placed this campaign was Fuller & Smith, in Chicago; the account executive was Clarence Madden. It was Madden who convinced Statler that he needed an advertising and promotion manager on his staff. Also, he had a candidate for the job — a young man named David Newton.

Newton had spent seven years in the 300-man advertising department of Sherwin-Williams Paint Company in Cleveland. He rose to the position of assistant director, his boss being Harry Dwight Smith who left to form the advertising agency of Fuller & Smith.

The Statler account was most important to the new agency and it behooved them to give to it the greatest attention and service. It was not an easy account to handle, for the client was a hardheaded and demanding man. Smith remembered the skill and energy of his assistant back at Sherwin-Williams and knew that if they could place him with Statler there should be advantages to all of them.

There was an initial reluctance on Statler's part. "Why should I hire him to work on my advertising? That's what *you* get paid for."

"It has always been my theory," Smith replied, "that brains are not so common in this world. Whenever we see a good one, I think it wise to buy it."

"You're right there," Statler admitted.

"Why don't you let Madden bring him out to Buffalo next weekend and see what you think of him."

"All right, all right! But I warn you, I'm not about to hire a man just to ease *your* job."

"I'm warned," Smith smiled.

Clarence Madden escorted a rather nervous David Newton to Statler's mansion on Soldiers Place one Sunday afternoon. As they turned into the driveway, flanked by towering poplar trees, Madden gave the young man a final bit of advice:

"He may bluster a bit, but don't be intimidated. It's a method he sometimes uses to test a man's guts. And, most important, if he asks something to which you don't know the answer, say so. Never, never try to bluff your way out because he'll spot it at once."

Statler himself opened the front door to greet them. After the introductions were performed, Madden drove off to leave the two alone. When they were settled in chairs, scotch and soda on the coffee table between them, Statler opened with his usual gambit:

"Well, young man, what do you have to say for yourself?"

It was a disconcerting question but Newton parried it skillfully. "Well, sir, the first thing I have to say for myself is that I don't know a thing about the hotel business."

"Thank God for that!" Statler cried and threw back his head in laughter. At the end of an hour Newton had been hired.

Newton developed an intuition on dealings with Statler. He knew when to fight for an idea and when not to, when to approach Statler by indirection and when head-on. He was given the house organ, *Statler Salesmanship*, to edit and was able to write articles and frame philosophies in Statler's own manner and style. David Newton became

Statler's alter-ego, a vice president, the third member of the "Big Four."

The final member was J. L. Hennessy, Chief Steward. He was quite different from his colleagues; different from the flexible McKowne, the stolid Stoner, the intuitive Newton; Hennessy was affable and non-competitive. He knew more about the mass purchase, storage, preparation and serving of food than any other single man in the business. He enjoyed his job immensely and saw no reason to get unduly involved in areas of management not his own. Since his word about the steward's department carried such enormous weight with Statler, he found no reason to say the words loudly or often.

There was the executive staff — the "Big Four" — Mc-Kowne, Stoner, Newton and Hennessy. They were trained in Statler's philosophy and methods, and bit by bit took from him the burdens of daily management.

It should have been time for Statler to know a feeling of accomplishment. He was a widely admired man, he had set the pattern of American hotels for years to come; he had given new dignity and new security to hotel labor; he was rich beyond Croesus. Yet, a dream of childhood still haunted him; the goal set by the thirteen-year-old bellhop at the McLure House in Wheeling had yet to be realized. He had vowed to himself he would one day own the largest hotel in the largest city of the world. New York was yet to be invaded and conquered.

CHAPTER 22

THE BIG TOWN

A rather curious little item appeared in the March 1916 issue of *Statler Salesmanship*:

> Hotel papers in various cities have been — and are — printing stories about a monster Hotel Statler in New York City. Don't get excited. These and other similar stories have this much foundation in fact: for more than a year real estate people, brokers, financiers and others have been trying to interest Mr. Statler in a hotel in New York. At the same time there have been propositions from a dozen — or a score — of other cities. And there's nothing definite to say about any of them. We can assume with reasonable certainty that a new Hotel Statler will be announced in time — whether it will be in New York or elsewhere no one — not even Mr. Statler — knows. Guessing is a lot of fun though — so long as it's understood that it's guessing.

It was not Statler's habit to display his uncertainties publicly. Perhaps this was a method of goading himself into making the big decision. In any event, it was clear that he was studying the New York scene with increasing attention.

A bit of news came to Buffalo that finally spurred him to action. The Pennsylvania Railroad announced that it was going to construct a new passenger terminal in New York at Seventh Avenue and 33rd Street, and perhaps a hotel directly across the street. He entrained at once for New York, spent a week inspecting the environs, and returned to Buffalo to discuss with his staff and directors what he had seen and heard.

His New York hotel acquaintances were almost unanimous in predicting disaster for any hotel located in that area. Seventh Avenue was the garment area, full of sweat shops. Thirty-fourth Street marked the edge of the Tenderloin District where vice and crime were a daily part of life. People simply would not patronize a hotel in this area; so they said.

Statler was not convinced, for he had seen a vision — he had seen the plans for the terminal drawn by McKim, Mead & White. Here was surely the epitome of an imperial railroad station. Entering from Seventh Avenue the traveler would find a long Roman arcade which held shops and restaurants; it ended in a grand staircase leading down to a colossal main hall inspired by the Imperial Roman Bath of Caracalla. There was majesty here, and no man could pass through it without feeling a lift of adventure.

The Pennsylvania Railroad would not build such an imposing structure without taking steps to improve the environment, Statler reasoned. Already the United States Post Office had been completed nearby; this, too, designed by McKim and having a facade of great columns to make it look like the Roman Forum. Millions of railroad dollars had been allocated to tear down nearby slums and to make access to secondary transportation systems. When the terminal was completed it would flood the area with travelers from New England, Long Island, the West, and from New Jersey via the Hudson Tube.

A major subway station was soon to be completed at Seventh Avenue and 34th Street, and this would make the Broadway theatre area easily accessible to the hotel's patrons. Convenience was the great plus; all a traveler would have to do when he stepped out of the terminal was walk across the street to the hotel. No taxis needed, no confusion, no baggage problem, a minimum of tipping.

Any hotel in this location would be a success, Statler decided. He picked up the phone and called Thomas W. Hulme, the railroad's vice president in charge of real estate and the hotel project.

"This is E. M. Statler and I'd like a chance to bid on the operating lease for your hotel."

"I'm sorry," Hulme said, "but I've promised the lease to another concern."

"Thank you," Statler said, and hung up. "Hell's delight!" he muttered angrily to himself. For the rest of that day his staff avoided him.

The following week the trade press carried the news that the operator of the hotel would be Franklin J. Matchette, a former president of the Milwaukee and Wisconsin Hotel Association. Statler tried to be charitable, but he couldn't help observing that the Pennsylvania people had called in a boy to do a man's job.

Apparently the Pennsylvania management had a second thought along that same line, for a month later Hulme asked Statler to come to New York for a conference. On December 11, 1916, Statler reported to his executives and his board of directors that the company had acquired the operating lease of the Hotel Pennsylvania now under construction. He was jubilant, as could be seen by the story in *Salesmanship*:

> There's big news from New York, just as we go to press. The world's biggest hotel — 2,200 rooms, 2,200 baths — is to be operated in the metropolis by Hotels Statler Company, Inc. . . . Mr. Statler closed the purchase of the operating lease on this property in December. The hotel was originally planned to be a 1,200-room structure but Mr. Statler arranged for two additional wings which will give it 1,000 more rooms — 2,200 in all.
>
> It will be the largest hotel in the world, for there is nothing now in existence or in course of construction that

has such a capacity . . . The architects and contractors are the men who built the mammoth Pennsylvania Station — McKim, Mead & White; and the George A. Fuller Company. The last-named firm were the general contractors for Hotel Statler, Detroit . . .

So here it comes! The long-expected, long-looked-forward-to New York hotel. Are we going to be ready for it? Are we going to be keen to embrace the promise it holds out? Are we going to be really active and important units in this big organization — growing with it, achieving with it, making the most of our opportunities and realizing our ambitions? Are we going to be *true* Statlerites — which means *doers*? Let's all make this the time to give ourselves a thorough going-over — and see what sort of fellows we are. Let's take inventory, and find out what this big accomplishment of our organization *really means to us*. And let's get on our toes and get ready.

The January 1917 issue of the house organ proclaimed:

The story of the latest addition to the Statler family — the great New York hotel — is on everybody's lips. The public is tremendously interested. Of course it created great enthusiasm within the Statler organization.

It's the great dream coming true!

Everybody sees that the New York house will be great in size — 2,200 rooms — 2,200 baths. Everyone will see, too, on a little thought — that it must be *great in service*.

Some details appeared in last month's *Salesmanship*. There you saw that it was opposite the Pennsylvania Railroad Station. Besides the Pennsylvania traffic there will come to this mammoth terminal express trains of the New York, New Haven & Hartford Railroad. There will be a great flow of people from New England and all points to the very doors of the new hotel — a location just where a multitude of people want a hotel. Placed where the four corners of the world's travel come together — this plot of ground, 400 by 200 feet, will have a hotel 16 stories above and three below the street level — representing $12,000,000.

The Gimbel Bros.' store . . . is on the east. It's a half

block to the Hudson tubes. There will be a new Seventh Avenue subway station in the hotel; new Broadway subway express station one block away; surface cars — elevated lines — in fact everything a New York visitor or resident can wish for is right at hand — including the bright lights of Herald Square a few steps away. Territory south will always be devoted largely to manufacturing — territory north will always hold a mercantile business.

Just as a sidelight the telephone contract, recently closed with the N. Y. Telephone Company, calls for the largest hotel switchboard — 24 positions — 200 trunk lines — $50,000 a year.

Breaking one record after another!

Excavation was begun last April.

The great question is the organization. This record-breaking hotel will demand an organization big and competent enough to make the *service* equal to the structure.

What did the New York hotel men (who had the habit of referring to Statler as "that man from Buffalo") think of his arrival in New York? They were, by and large, silent. But not the trade press — it was exuberant. The *Daily Hotel Reporter* in New York City wrote:

He said he would do it — and he did it! We welcome you to our city, Mr. Statler.

Hotel Review commented:

E. M. Statler, president of Hotels Statler Company, while visiting New York during the recent National Hotel Men's Exposition, remarked that some day he was going to open a hotel in New York, and then he would show some of the bonifaces of the metropolis a thing or two about the great and intricate profession of hotel keeping which they had missed through their lack of experience and years.

Mr. Statler's friends laughed with him over what they considered a bit of pleasantry, and promptly forgot his statement. When, therefore, it was announced that the controlling interest in the lease of the new Pennsylvania Hotel had been sold to E. M. Statler by Franklin J. Matchette there was a great recalling of Mr. Statler's words at the Exposition, and a grand "Sure, I knew he'd do it — didn't he say he would?" . . .

However, whether "they" suspected it or not the old veteran of the catering game has advanced his holdings to the metropolis and in the usual Statler style he bargained for and obtained the biggest proposition obtainable . . .

Statler has always been one of us, and a prime good fellow, who will feel quite at home here in New York as the lessee of what will be one of the world's greatest hotels. Statler has a nationwide reputation as a student of the service and art of both building and conducting hotels. It is not only his business but also, as one's business should be, a hobby. He is an enthusiast, a lover of his work, gifted with a highly developed imagination, the sort to which so many kings of finance and commerce owe their standing in the world. To say that he will be welcomed in New York would be simply to state the obvious. To predict for him another tremendous success, even unto the business regeneration of the entire Pennsylvania terminal neighborhood, is but to echo the conviction of all who are acquainted with him and his work.

The *Mid-West Hotel Reporter* stated:

Statler the Startler proved his clear title to that appellation again last week when the announcement came from him that he had taken over the lease to the big New York City hotel . . . originally leased to F. J. Matchette . . . The working out of Mr. Statler's plans seems the natural and quite automatic result of a system or method of hotel operating efficiency devised by himself and therefore peculiar to himself. The word genius is appropriately applied to E.M. for it fits him like the proverbial glove.

Despite the hurrahs and the accolades from the trade press, there were to be a couple of hitches in this operation. Statler had never before entered into just this kind of a deal, nor would he ever again.

CHAPTER 23

THE NEW YORK STATLER

The complicated financial and management arrangements for the operation of the Pennsylvania Hotel had many built-in human stresses. For a smooth conduct of business the greatest forbearance and patience was required among the principals — and none of the three (Matchette, Hulme and Statler) had these qualities.

The New York Hotel Statler Company was organized and issued 40,000 shares of voting common stock. Matchette held 10,000 of it, Statler 30,000. The agreement with Matchette also provided for the issuance of preferred stock at $100 per share. Statler, through his Buffalo company, purchased $2,000,000 worth of the preferred and thereby held safe financial control.

Matchette didn't think very highly of the stock in any event, and since the Pennsylvania Railroad had forced him to relinquish control of the project, he was determined that the hotel should return him a good percentage on his money. He insisted that any profit shown by the hotel should be distributed in stock dividends.

This ran contrary to Statler's temperament, to his concept of sound business practices. He could not stand having unpaid obligations and he planned to pay off the corporation's bonded indebtedness before any profits were distributed. Under the agreement between them, Matchette had the right to examine the corporation's books. He exercised that right vigorously, and each time gave forth with loud lamentations about the way the money was being used.

NEW YORK STATLER

Mr. Statler's "grand hotel" was the 2,200-room Hotel Pennsylvania, now the Statler-Hilton. Opened in January 1919 as a virtual "city within a city" and the world's largest hotel, it provided over 1,000 modern rooms at modest prices for salesmen and also had luxurious suites, a palatial first floor ballroom with its own street entrance, and an exotic roof-garden restaurant. By tunnel, the hotel is connected to Penn Station, the Long Island Railroad, the city's subways, and Gimbel's department store. Shown below is the hotel's original enormous lobby.

STATLER HOTELS

In 1928, there were Statler Hotels in Boston, Buffalo, Cleveland, Detroit, and St. Louis that provided a total of 7,250 modern rooms, all with bath. Following Mr. Statler's death in 1928, the Pittsburgh and Washington hotels were added, and after 1950, the Los Angeles, Hartford, and Dallas Statlers were built. In 1954, the hotel system was merged with Hilton Hotels. Early Statler Hotels were all located in major cities linked by Eastern railroads.

STAY *Hote*

Chicago Office ★

D

ST. LOUIS

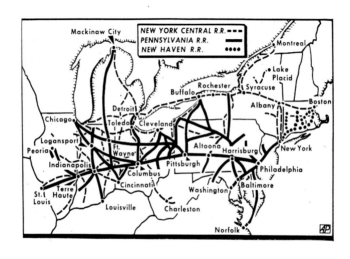

NEW YORK CENTRAL R.R.	- - -
PENNSYLVANIA R.R.	——
NEW HAVEN R.R.	••••

TATLER WHEN YOU VISIT

BOSTON

BUFFALO

NEW YORK
Formerly
Hotel Pennsylvania

CLEVELAND

PITTSBURGH
Hotel William Penn

WASHINGTON

Printed in U.S.A. by THE STATLER PRESS
Courtesy Buffalo & Erie County Historical Society

E. M. Statler was America's foremost hotelman when this photograph was taken in 1925.

Mr. Statler looks leeward in this photograph, taken aboard his yacht, the Miramar. An avid fisherman, he also liked golf, that of the fairways, and the "indoor golf" of management.

LIFE IS SERVICE - THE ONE WHO PROGRESSES IS THE ONE WHO GIVES HIS FELLOW MEN A LITTLE MORE - A LITTLE BETTER SERVICE

Plaque on Statler Hall, home of Cornell's School of Hotel Administration, commemorates Mr. Statler's philosophy.

"He's a damned meddler," Statler announced to his secretary after one of Matchette's stormy visits. "Don't let him in my office any more. I'm not going to see him."

Having banished Matchette, Statler repurchased $200,-000 worth of the bonds in 1919, and by the fall of 1921 he had called in the remainder. Now he was ready to pay dividends, and they were considerable.

Statler was not able to solve his problems with Thomas Hulme quite so easily, though in the end he used much the same technique. The trouble between these stemmed simply from the fact that Hulme was the boss. Statler didn't own the hotel, the railroad did. He was to pay them $1,000,000 a year rental, which was all right with him, but for that money he didn't want the railroad to give him any advice on the construction or operation of the hotel. And that was exactly what Hulme proceeded to do. Perhaps not really advice — it was more like orders.

There was a series of monumental collisions between these two, starting back when the plans were still on the drawing table. The first issue was about the size of the rooms. The luxury hotels in New York such as the Ritz Carlton and the Plaza, had spacious guestrooms with high ceilings. Hulme wanted to follow the tradition, but Statler insisted that it was uneconomic; the high-ceilinged rooms were hard to heat and cut down on the number of rooms that could be contained in the building. He was aiming at 2,200 rooms (the largest in the world) and he would not be swerved from the goal. Statler won this one.

For additional income Statler wanted street-level stores in the hotel facing on Seventh Avenue. Hulme objected on the grounds that stores would cheapen the appearance of the world's largest hotel. Hulme won the first round on this one — the stores were not added until later.

The size of the lobby was cause for dissension. Hulme wanted a vast lobby, something on the order of Penn Station's grand concourse. Statler objected to the waste of space that could be used for income-producing rooms. "The lobby must be impressive," Hulme insisted. He won.

Statler took a stand against the design of the main entrance on Seventh Avenue. "It would be fine for a cathedral," he said, "but not for a hotel. Let's get the people in, not scare them away." He won.

There was a fifty percent chance, or better, that Statler could win any argument with Hulme, but he considered it a terrible waste of time. At last he decided to treat Hulme the same way he treated Matchette — pretend he didn't exist.

As the great hotel began to take shape Statler could be seen roaming the floors, blueprints under his arm, issuing orders to change this or change that or change the other thing. Most of the changes were completed before Hulme could discover and countermand them. It was a time of great frustration for him; a railroad was never run *this* way.

Bernard Gimbel of Gimbel Brothers had a department store just east on Broadway, and he came to Statler with a project. "What the railroad and your hotel need is easy access to Broadway," he said. "You're a bit isolated over there on Seventh Avenue and you need to encourage traffic in that direction."

"How do you propose to do it?"

"You need an easy, all-weather access to Broadway. My idea is to build a pedestrian tunnel from the Penn terminal straight east to Broadway. Such a tunnel would connect up with your hotel, with the BMT and IRT subways, the Hudson tube to New Jersey, the Long Island Railroad and, finally, with my store on Broadway. It would be beneficial to all of us, including the public."

"Hell's fire! Let's do it!" Statler slapped the table before him. Then he paused in thought a moment, perhaps remembering his auditor Stoner. "Who would pay for the tunnel?" he asked.

"The Pennsylvania Railroad," Gimbel said promptly.

Statler grinned. "Let's go see Hulme."

Hulme was convinced. The tunnel was dug and paid for by the railroad. The tunnel played no small role in the modernization and prosperity that came to that midtown area that was once part of Hell's Kitchen.

During the building of the hotel, Statler arranged for a temporary cafeteria to be installed in the basement for the use of the construction workers. The food was free and therefore the place was well patronized, not only by the masons and electricians and carpenters and structural steel workers, but also by a number of neighborhood derelicts who wandered in off the street.

James Janis had been placed in charge of the place, along with instructions from Statler not to be too hard on the bums if they were really hungry. He didn't want them to become regular guests but they were not to be grudged an occasional meal.

After a week of operation one of the service men came to Janis and said, "There's one bum that's been freeloading on us every day since we opened. I think it's time we kicked him out."

"Where is he?" Janis asked.

"Right over there on the bench, the guy in the rumpled suit."

Janis laughed. "Well, you can forget right now about throwing him out. That's Mr. Statler."

After recovery from his surprise the man exclaimed, "What in hell is he doing eating down here?"

"Beats me," Janis said.

What Statler was doing was listening. He had discovered that workmen tend to shoptalk during the lunch break and he was there to hear their opinions of the construction. If any of the subcontractors were chiseling on material, not living up to the specifications, sooner or later he'd hear gossip about it at lunch. And woe to the contractor!

Brick by brick, Statler was turning the Pennsylvania into a *Statler* hotel with all the construction and service innovations he had pioneered over the years. He came up with something new as well. It was something invented by Matchette and designed to give the guests more room privacy and eliminate a lot of tipping. All his life Statler had opposed (unsuccessfully) the custom of tipping. Here was a chance for him to relieve the guests of some of this annoyance.

The device was called a Servidor and consisted of a wide, bulging panel on both the inside and outside of the guest-room door. The panels were hinged and locked separately upon the door itself. If the guest had any pressing or cleaning to be done he opened the Servidor from the inside, placed the garments in the chamber revealed, then closed and locked his panel. The bellman or porter would remove the garments by opening the outside panel. The reverse was performed when the clothing was returned; the bellman placing the garment in the chamber from the outside, and the guest removing it at his convenience from the inside. No intrusion of privacy, no tip for the service.

The public enthusiasm for this door was great. Statler was flooded with letters of praise and thanks from grateful guests. One of the most interesting came from an elderly traveler from the Mid-West who wanted to buy one. He wrote:

> I don't know how it works, but it does. My daughter told me to put my suit in there and it would be cleaned and pressed. And it was. So, where do I get one to take home?

When the hotel was nearing completion Statler met and liked a general practitioner by the name of Dr. J. Darwin Nagel. Nagel was a great raconteur and regaled

Statler with medical stories. One evening, when they were both part of a poker game, Nagel said:

"Why don't you install a complete medical department in your new hotel?"

Statler did not ordinarily permit extraneous subjects to interrupt his poker game, but this idea intrigued him. He rubbed his chin. "I hadn't thought of it," he admitted.

"There is nothing more frightening than to be sick while away from home and among strangers."

"I know," Statler said ruefully.

"If you had a complete medical center in the hotel, including X-ray and surgical room, your guests could receive immediate and understanding attention."

"Put it on paper and give it to me," Statler said.

Nagel put it on paper and Statler approved of the idea. The Pennsylvania became the first hotel in history to offer its guests such broad medical service. Statler gave Nagel space on the tenth floor, equi-distant from top and bottom, and the doctor organized his department to include, besides himself, a head nurse, four regular nurses, a night nurse and a night physician, and all the most modern equipment. Some time later Statler added a dentist — Dr. W. F. Randolph. No other hotel in the world could match this service. Statler quipped, "We got 'em in sickness and in health."

As the Pennsylvania was pushed to completion during the closing months of 1918, New Yorkers became fascinated with every detail of the "biggest hotel in the world." David Newton ground out press releases that were eagerly received and printed by the newspapers, mere statistics of bigness being considered newsworthy.

Newton wrote about the kitchen:

"The Pennsylvania kitchen will contain $1,000,000 worth of equipment in its 25,000 feet of floor space . . . The chef's staff will consist of 9 bakers, 10 pastry bakers, 4 ice cream chefs, 9 butchers, 12 cold meat cooks, 9 roast cooks, 12 sauce cooks, 9 fry cooks, 6 vegetable girls, 4 soup cooks, 4 banquet chefs, 8 pot washers, 4 cleaners . . ."

The social and political climate of New York was exactly right for Statler's project. The war was ending and the people were tired of idealism and sacrifice. They were to elect Warren Harding President of the United States on his platform of "back to normalcy." Normalcy meant a variety of things to a variety of people, to most it meant *fun!* Statler's hotel was designed for fun.

On the morning of January 25, 1919, the *New York Times* carried a feature story that was headlined:

WORLD'S BIGGEST HOTEL
OPENS TODAY!
THE PENNSYLVANIA, WITH 2,200 ROOMS,
2,200 BATHS,

READY FOR GUESTS

The article continued:

> The incandescent skyline of the heart of New York received a big addition to its candlepower last night when, on the gloomiest offshoot of Times Square, hundreds of windows were illuminated in the largest tavern in the world, the Hotel Pennsylvania, which has its public opening today.
>
> Seventh Avenue which had been practically in the hands of the receiver during the years of subway building began to look again as if it belonged to Manhattan.
>
> The second-hand men and curb brokers in clothing who have long predominated between Times Square and Pennsylvania Station stood on the sidewalk and in their shop doors last night looking at the outlines of the great structure with apprehension on their faces, expressive of the fear that the autonomous development of their lowly traffic in the heart of New York was seriously threatened. . . .
>
> The Hotel Pennsylvania will give New York its first experience with the Statler Hotel management and service. E. M. Statler, who directs the chain of Hotels Statler at

Buffalo, Cleveland, Detroit and St. Louis, will be in charge of the Hotel Pennsylvania and will run it in accordance with his own ideas.

Anyone under the impression that, because he has heard of the Statler management as an introducer of many novelties, the Pennsylvania is to be a sort of trick hotel will be disappointed. It was stated last night by a representative of the company that the art of managing hotels had been carried to such a point of perfection that any radical variations were likely to be unsuccessful.

One feature which will have its first metropolitan trial in the Hotel Pennsylvania is the Servidor. This is a small wardrobe which is built into the bedroom doors. The guest may open it from the inside and put his shoes or clothing into it. They will be noiselessly extracted by an attendant from the outside, and returned shined and pressed. . . . The purpose of this device is to make frequent and unreasonable visits of bellboys unnecessary. . . .

Clerks and other employees, it is asserted will be stocked with information about New York streets and transportation systems, and the merits of different shows and other topics of interest to visitors. . . .

The night of the opening Statler had 2,000 guests; they were New York's VIP's, civic, social and business leaders, along with the press. Before sitting down to the most sumptuous banquet the million-dollar kitchen could prepare, they were taken on a tour of the establishment. The *New York Times* was again impressed by size and variety. It wrote:

> . . . sixty girls will be required to operate the hotel telephone exchange with its 200 trunk lines . . . A few of the special features for the guests include a library of 4,000 volumes, Turkish baths and swimming pools for men and women, and a roof garden. At the entrance to each restaurant in the hotel is a sign reading, "This checking service is free — you are not expected to tip."

What the *Times* did not find newsworthy was that Statler had hired a rather unknown band and installed it in the hotel's Grill Room. The band leader's name was Vincent Lopez and he played such tunes as *The Sheik of Araby*, *Ain't We Got Fun?*, *Smiles*, and *Makin' Whoopee*. The curtain was rising on the "Jazz Age," and Statler was ready.

A post-war business slump hit the nation shortly after this opening, and many hotels and hotel chains went into bankruptcy. But not Statler's Pennsylvania. From the first day until the great depression ten years later, the Pennsylvania remained 90 percent occupied. After paying the $1,000,000 rental to the railroad each year, Statler still had an annual net profit of 2 to 3 million dollars. During those years the Pennsylvania made more money than any other hotel in New York.

The country cousin had shown the city boys a thing or two.

CHAPTER 24

THE BEST OF EVERYTHING

Prior to his success in New York Statler had doggedly resisted giving himself any laurels. Whatever the hotel industry said about him, he knew he was not a complete success until his childhood dream had become reality. Now it had. He had scaled the peak and wherever he looked there were valleys of toiling men. He had made it at 56 years of age. Could he reasonably expect more from life? He *had* expected more.

Perhaps every spectacularly successful man finds an unexpected emptiness at his greatest moment. For Statler, the aspect of life that dismayed and defeated him was his relationship with his family. He was simply not a successful father, and the harder he tried the greater his failures.

He adopted four children — Milton, Marian, Elva and Ellsworth — put them in a mansion, surrounded them with a housekeeper, governess, assistant governess, upstairs maid, parlor maid, butler, two cooks, gardener and a chauffeur. He left instructions they were to have "the best of everything." The *best?* That word was interpreted as meaning tangible things — swimming pools and parties, ponies and carts, motor cars and yachts.

How strange it was that Statler, who attributed his own success to hard work, seemed blind to his own children's need of this vital ingredient for self-respect and happiness. He wanted his children to have it better than he had had, and what he gave them was worse.

From time to time, when he observed laziness or self-indulgence developing in his children, he imposed upon them a stern program of self-improvement. The two oldest children felt the main brunt; Milton was instructed to learn typing and shorthand, Marian to play the piano and organ.

After the construction of the Pennsylvania Hotel, Statler spent the major part of each week in New York, coming home to Buffalo for long weekends. Immediately upon his arrival each Friday he would summon the children before him and quiz them on the progress they had made during the week. He inquired of Milton how many words a minute he could type and upon hearing the number, demanded that the child do it now so he might inspect the work. And if Milton failed to perform up to his rather optimistic report, there followed a lecture.

As for Marian, she was required to give a concert on the great organ in the front hall so that he might judge her progress and thereby measure her application.

After parcelling out praise and criticism with careful justice Statler would grab up his golf clubs and go off to play with his Buffalo cronies. This was not a homecoming but an inspection, and the children came to dread each Friday.

Since Statler expected his home to run with the efficiency of his hotels, the weekends were not happy times for the servants either. Of all the people in the house the only one truly eager for the master's arrival was his wife. His appearance in her third-floor suite provided a welcome break in the drab days of her self-imposed exile. He ordered dinner and champagne for two to be served with candlelight in her parlor. First he drank a toast to her, and then he recounted the details of his week in New York. He frequently solicited an opinion from her about a management or personnel problem. Between courses he put on a phonograph record and they danced.

He made no comments about her strange passiveness,

nor about the long march of gin bottles in and out of her room during the week. The doctors had been unable to make a diagnosis on her withdrawal from life and he wasn't going to try. He thought the kindest thing he could do was to act toward her as if nothing had changed.

Statler loved his children — in his way. His way was to treat them as adults, as if they were capable of self-discipline and moderation. When they went to excesses he was bewildered and hurt. He never spanked them; his discipline consisted of the silent treatment. He assumed that this would shame them, make them change their ways in order to win back father's approval. It didn't work that way, however. Frequently the children didn't know what they had done to offend father, and since he was not speaking to them there was no way of discovering their transgressions.

At a very young age the children learned there was an unvarying pattern: the silence always ended with a gift. The longer the silence the greater the gift. It was as if father was the guilty one and the gift an apology.

In the confusion between acceptance and rejection, discipline and permissiveness, the children could turn only to the governess, Anna Boyer. No one could have played the role better than Anna, an uncomplicated young woman from Syracuse. She had never traveled any place before getting this job, never had been exposed to wealth or to the dark emotions it seemed to engender, but she had one gyro that stabilized her in this alien environment — she loved the children who were given to her care.

It was on her lap they climbed to hear the nursery stories, on her shoulder they cried with fear or frustration. She never lost her temper, her arms were always open, she was the one constant element in their young lives. But she was not their mother, she could not take the place of a mother. She had the privilege to love, but not the permission to discipline, and without the two there could be no real security for the children. And so they grew up as best they could.

Milton, the eldest of the children (born in 1910), was Statler's hope for the future and he looked forward to the day when Milton would be president of the great hotel empire. This dream was not shattered by any single event; it simply eroded away over the painful years.

There was not a hotel opening that did not find Milton beside Statler all during the festivities. First he was a baby in arms and introduced by the father as "Honey Boy." Then he was a boy in knee pants, smiling engagingly from the speakers' table at opening banquets. As a nine-year-old he ceremoniously signed the Pennsylvania register and became the very first guest. The metropolitan newspapers carried pictures of the event and the statement of the proud father: "Already he's a hotel man."

After his formal education was completed, Milton found himself wearing a pair of overalls and working in the Pennsylvania boiler room. When he complained to his father that he had expected a better job, Statler snapped, "You're going to learn this business from the ground up."

A few months later Milton was put in the kitchen. He was a handsome and personable young man, but a practical joker, a hell-raiser. After a week's time on this new job, the chef came to Statler to complain that Milton had just about destroyed all discipline in his department. Though he didn't say it right out, the implication was that either he or Milton would have to leave. Statler telephoned an old friend who was manager of the Commodore Hotel and requested that he take Milton in his kitchen. For the next few months Milton commuted from the Pennsylvania to the Commodore kitchen and back in his new yellow Stutz Bearcat.

The chef at the Commodore soon reached the end of his patience with Milton's hijinks and the young man returned to the Pennsylvania as an assistant manager. Statler had vowed to promote the boy only as he earned it, but instead he promoted him out of desperation.

This time the father enlisted the aid of a bell captain, an old and faithful employee named Charles Ashbaugh. "Charlie," Statler said to him, "I want you to look out for Milton and keep him on the right path. See that he does his job and does it right. You see him more than I do around here and he may listen to you. Keep him working all the time, and for God's sake, keep him sober on the job."

"Mister Statler," Ashbaugh said, "he's doing fine. He's a very nice boy and everyone likes him and he's doing fine."

"Really?" Statler exclaimed with a pathetic eagerness. "You mean it, Charlie?"

"I sure do."

"Well, look after him, and God bless you."

Charlie Ashbaugh was overly optimistic. Milton was gay and charming and just wouldn't stay sober, no matter how the older man reasoned or threatened. Charlie faithfully looked after the boy, but his duties too often consisted of carrying him to bed, drunk.

Late one summer Statler heard indirectly that Milton had expressed a desire to study law. By now he had faced the fact that Milton would not succeed in the hotel business, and he even speculated that perhaps the boy's dislike of it was the reason for his drinking so heavily. If he wanted to be a lawyer, great! Through intermediaries, Statler arranged for his son to enroll in New York University. When the boy showed up and actually signed for the course and put down the tuition fee, Statler was thrilled — so thrilled he wanted to celebrate the event by a gift.

Milton had long wanted a boat, and now he received one. His father took him to a marina in the East River and pointed to a sleek and glittering Chris-Craft. It was his.

Such was Milton's delight in the boat, and the fascination he felt for the world of water, he never got around to attending the law classes.

"Did I do wrong?" Statler demanded of his wife in anguish. "If I had not given him the boat would he have gone into law?"

"I don't know, dear," she said softly.

The situation brought about another confrontation between father and son. Statler spoke in controlled anger, counting off the boy's failures, his drunkenness, and demanded that he reform.

At the end of the tirade, Milton looked directly at his father and said, "You let me do a lot of things you shouldn't have when I was a kid. Now it's too late to change me."

There was a terrible stab of truth in what the boy had said. Statler turned away from him, tears in his eyes.

Statler's wife, Mary Manderbach Statler, died during October 1925 in the family suite on the sixteenth floor of the Pennsylvania Hotel. She had not wanted to move to New York; she knew she could not be a hostess for her husband and she feared her presence might embarrass him, that he would be ashamed of her. This was not the case. Had it been, Statler would simply have acceded to her wishes and left her in Buffalo. He had a great fondness for her, as well as a feeling of responsibility. He insisted that she be with him so he could look after her. Her death was slow and agonizing; the disease was cancer.

Had she been drinking so heavily because of the pain? If so, who could blame her?

CHAPTER 25

MISS ALICE SEIDLER

A man is comforted best by one who makes no demand upon him, either for tears or bravery or gloomy discussion, but gives the balm of compassionate silence. Statler received this from a gentle-spoken woman named Alice Seidler; she had been his private secretary since November 1918. He had hired her with some misgivings.

Alice Seidler had been an editorial secretary at *Life*, the old humor magazine, and when she observed it sinking deeper in red ink she knew it was time for her to find another job. She passed the construction site of the Pennsylvania Hotel on her way to work each day and it occurred to her that there might be some secretarial jobs available when the structure was finished. She wrote a letter of application to the "Manager" of the hotel and to her surprise received a prompt answer instructing her to come for an interview at 3 o'clock on the following day.

She arrived promptly and was met by Frank McKowne who said, "Come with me, please. I want you to meet Mr. Statler." They entered a room on the unfinished mezzanine floor and found several men bending over a drawing board spread with blueprints.

"Mr. Statler," McKowne said, "Could you take a moment to interview this young lady?"

"What for?"

"A position as your secretary."

Statler slammed down a ruler and cried, "Damn it, McKowne, I don't have time to interview anybody. And besides, I don't need a secretary. Now get her out of here."

When Alice Seidler got back to her office at *Life* she told a friend where she had been. "You can't work in a hotel," the girl exclaimed. "No respectable woman works in a hotel."

Alice smiled ruefully. "That is something we won't have to worry about."

Though she didn't know it, Alice Seidler had been briefly caught in the middle of a running dispute between Statler and his executives. Statler had no private secretary of his own and was in the habit of dictating massive correspondence to whomever he happened upon during his walks through the offices of his staff. This not only tended to disrupt the routine of the department, but also made for some confusion in his own correspondence.

Though McKowne had pressured him to hire a secretary of his own, Statler had stubbornly refused. He would willingly have doubled the kitchen staff but he begrudged each typist added to the executive payroll because he did not see any direct contribution they made to the comfort of the guests. As for taking on his own personal secretary, he considered it as self-indulgence and display.

In his heart he knew he was wrong; he knew that his Spartan regimen, intended to set the pattern for his subordinates, had resulted in much inefficiency. He meant to do something about it when he got around to it, but he would not be pushed. There was some surprise, therefore, when he grumbled to McKowne the following week that he might as well have a talk with that girl who had interrupted him in his work.

When McKowne put through a call to Alice Seidler it was she who now held back. She was not at all certain she wished to work for a man as rude as Mr. Statler. Under urging, she agreed to come for an interview the following day.

On this occasion Statler greeted her with courtesy and charm. He smiled at her, pulled up a chair for her, and obliquely apologized for his previous conduct by explaining the great amount of work he had to do. The brief amenities over, he gave her a pencil and a pad of paper and at a rapid pace began to dictate a letter. It was addressed to her:

Miss Seidler:

In further reference to your application to me for the position of my personal secretary-stenographer, it will be necessary for me to know your belief in your own qualifications and ability to do the following things and produce the following results.

First, and most important, to be able to control an unruly, unsystematic, disorderly, inefficient business man — one who has never, regularly, for any length of time stayed at his desk, and make out of him, for at least a few hours a day, the reverse of the above.

Second, to see that I make engagements for a definite, specific hour and in such order in sequence that neither my time nor the time of others is wasted.

Third, to help me plan certain hours for certain work and TO SEE that I carry out my plan.

Fourth, to answer letters cleverly, tactfully, diplomatically, graciously, in a few words and right to the point from rough, crude notes on the same.

Fifth, to be able TO SEE, after reading correspondence, the necessity for further information on the subject therein and to either assemble such information, before presenting to me, or present same to me with evidence that such information is being secured, and will be presented in due time.

Sixth, to be able to keep records and trace ALL letters and orders to their finality in proper time.

Seventh, to be willing to forget time and hours, if necessary, during the completion and opening period of the hotel, and until our work is properly organized and systematized.

Eighth and finally, to be able to INSIST regardless of the possibility of my putting it off or shirking, that certain things must be done NOW.

If you feel capable of successfully handling the tasks here outlined, you may say so in your own way on the bottom or on the back of this letter, and state when you will be able to begin this work.

Yours very truly,

Alice Seidler transcribed the letter from her notes, made a few terse comments on her own on the back of it, placed it on Statler's desk and left. Two days later a call came from McKowne.

"Mr. Statler thinks you're a little slow," he said.

"Mr. Statler dictates a little fast," she replied.

There was a moment of uncertain silence on the other end of the wire, then McKowne said, "Well, Mr. Statler says you can come to work but on your own responsibility."

"No one has ever guaranteed me anything," she replied. "I'll report on Monday morning."

Statler had never had a private secretary before and he approached the relationship with some misgiving. He had known men who were, in his opinion, hag-ridden by their secretaries and he was determined to have none of that. Strangely, the very qualities he had demanded of Alice Seidler in the letter, ". . . to be able to control an unruly, unsystematic, disorderly, inefficient business man . . ." were the things he would fight against. He had listed them as a warning that the job would not be easy.

There was something else about this soft-spoken, thirty-six-year-old woman that gave him pause. She seemed to have complete self-possession, the kind that comes from a background of wealth and social position. "Probably a college woman," he snorted to himself. "Bryn Mawr, or something like that."

He was not afraid of being patronized by this woman, experts had attempted that, but he feared she would find the hotel business dull. There was one thing he demanded above all else from the people around him — enthusiasm! If she didn't have that, out she'd go!

Statler misread Alice Seidler at that first meeting. The self-possession which he attributed to snobbism was nothing of the sort; it was the quiet confidence of a woman who had surmounted personal tragedy. She had known both affluence and poverty, and was impressed by neither.

In 1882, the year of her birth, the family home was a large brownstone on Hudson Street, in Hoboken, New Jersey. It was a fashionable neighborhood and behind their house was the stable which held a matched pair of geldings and a glittering carriage with fringed canopy. Henry Seidler had a good position with the Pullman Company, designing much of their equipment, and he supported his large family (seven children by his first wife who died, and two children by Ellen, his second wife) in great style. Alice was the youngest of them all, and most of her half-brothers and sisters had married and moved away by the time of the tragedy.

The Pullman car interiors, with crystal and brass and inlaid woods and rich upholstery, were setting new standards of luxury travel and making the company a great deal of money. Henry Seidler's friends insisted that since his designs were making the company rich, he deserved a better contract. He was making a large salary already and was content, but under their prodding it finally became a question of pride — he felt that he had to ask for a better contract or appear a weakling and a fool.

At contract renewal time he presented a demand for almost double the fee. The company not only rejected his demands, they cancelled his contract entirely. That day Henry Seidler did not come home until very late, and then he did not come into the house. He very carefully opened the ornamental iron gate, closed it behind him, and walked down the side of the house to enter the stable.

There he put a gun to his head and pulled the trigger.

He was unsuccessful in the suicide attempt — he merely blinded himself.

Poverty moved in at once. Seidler had lived up to his income and when he stopped working there was nothing to cushion the family. The brownstone house went, as did the matched pair of horses and the gleaming carriage. The family moved into a mean flat and existed on the charity of relatives.

Until she was old enough to go to work, Alice's dresses were all hand-me-downs from distant cousins. Her mother washed and scrubbed and took in roomers, surrendering the family privacy. The blind father spent most of each day building birdcages of cigar boxes. Alice came directly home from school each afternoon to read biographies aloud to her father until dinnertime.

Yet it was not a gloomy home. Ellen, the mother, set the tone by living each day with briskness and good nature. She was determined that her children should not grow up with a feeling of inferiority, of self-pity. And they didn't. Even her husband recovered from his despair and faced the long march of black and featureless days with courage and even laughter.

Alice was both the youngest and the most responsible of all the children. At fourteen years of age she announced that she was quitting school in order to study typing and shorthand during the evenings at a nearby business school. She chose evenings so that she could continue reading to her father during the day.

At fifteen she obtained a stenographic job with a law firm in Manhattan and began proudly to contribute to the support of her father and mother. She continued to do so during their lifetimes.

She was thirty-six when she went to work for the fifty-six-year-old hotel tycoon.

With their backgrounds so similar it was remarkable

how little they understood each other at the beginning. The reason was, perhaps, that they had faced poverty quite differently — he with open battle, she with quiet resolution.

There must always be a period of adjustment between boss and secretary, but in this case it was doubly difficult because of the divergence of methods and personalities. Alice Seidler had never worked for a man with such explosive energy and such impatience. He had never had an employee with such quiet independence. She thought him crude, he thought her passive and snobbish. It seemed a question of which would happen first — whether he'd fire her or she'd quit. Somehow, neither happened. They continued together until each began to appreciate the qualities of the other. The most important discovery that Statler made was that his new secretary had good judgment.

She had been with him little more than a month when the New York Hotel Association scheduled a luncheon meeting. Its purpose was to adopt some policies to which Statler objected.

That morning Statler grumbled about the loss of time the meeting would cause him. "But I've got to go and set those goddamn fools straight," he said.

Alice Seidler, sitting across the office from him remained silent.

"Well, what are you objecting to?" he demanded.

"I didn't say a word, Mr. Statler," she replied.

"You don't have to. I can tell when you dissapprove of something. All right, speak up. What were you thinking?"

"I was thinking that if I were you I'd be careful what I said out there. You're new to New York and you may make some enemies if you presume to lecture them."

"Horsefeathers!" Statler snorted, and walked out of the office.

He returned late that afternoon, threw his hat at the filing cabinet and his body at the desk chair. "Well, Miss

Seidler, do you want to hear what happened at the meeting?"

"Yes, sir."

"I kept my mouth shut, that's what happened. It wasn't easy but I did it. It was good advice you gave me."

As his respect for her common sense and discretion grew, he used her more and more as his intelligence arm and as a buffer. Several times a week he'd ask her help in smoothing a rough spot in the organization. He'd say, "Miss Seidler, I hear that the fry chef has some sort of grievance. I wish you'd go talk to him and find out what it's all about. I could go, but I think he'll talk more freely to you."

When she'd report back, he'd demand not only the facts but her opinion on what was to be done. More often than not he agreed with her.

After a year on the job she asked, not surprisingly, for a raise. Statler was a little offended. Like most generous and paternalistic employers, he liked to think that he was more concerned about his employees' welfare than they were themselves. He considered himself a father image (which he was) with the responsibilities and privileges of parenthood. To question his decision on wages or hours or working conditions was to be an ungrateful child, a naughty child.

The truth was that Statler's wages and benefits were far higher than the industry average. That Alice Seidler's salary was not in keeping with her duties and responsibilities was a fact that he had somehow overlooked. He did not enjoy having this called to his attention.

When she asked for the raise he frowned at his desk for a long moment, trying to find a defense, a counterattack. At last he said, a little lamely, "You're very slow, Miss Seidler."

"Slow? You mean a slow typist?"

"Yes, that's exactly what I mean," he said with new firmness. "You're slow on the typewriter."

She was not at all disconcerted by his statement of an incontrovertible fact. "Well, Mr. Statler, you'll have to decide whether you want an expert machine operator or someone who can handle your routine correspondence without your having to dictate each letter."

She said no more, nor did he. There were many more cogent reasons for the raise, but she confined herself to the minor issue he had introduced. The following week she got her raise, and a little more too.

There was one issue between them that was never completely solved — his language. One day she said to him, "Mr. Statler, there is one thing you do that hurts me; you use the name of the Deity to emphasize your points. I'm not accustomed to hearing such profanity."

It is interesting to speculate how Statler would have responded had anyone else made that criticism. Certainly it would have been with some more use of the Deity's name. In this case, however, he gave thoughtful consideration to the point. After a moment he said, "I'll tell you what. Every time I swear, you throw your inkwell at me."

It was not a serious proposal, but it was an elusive promise to try and restrain his language. He did rather well for a time, but there came a conference with some linen suppliers who wanted to increase the price of sheets. She had been on an errand and, returning to the office, she heard his angry and profane harangue a good twenty-five yards away. After the suppliers had left, defeated, she said, "You know, I could hear your language way down in the mezzanine."

"Miss Seidler, there are some men you can't make an impression on any other way. Besides," he grinned at her, "my language has been better lately, hasn't it? I mean, when I don't have any sons-of-bitches to deal with."

CHAPTER 26

BACK TO BUFFALO

Those close to Statler began to recognize the symptoms during the closing days of 1919. He was preoccupied and a little short-tempered; he tended to pace up and down the Pennsylvania lobby while eating an orange, putting the peelings in his pocket; he was forever misplacing his cheap, battered hat and sending the bellboys in search of it. He was clearly having an interior dialogue and this could mean but one thing — he was about to build another hotel.

Not only did the subjective symptoms indicate this, but so did the objective facts on the company ledgers. Money was pouring in from the Buffalo, Cleveland, Detroit and St. Louis hotels, and the Pennsylvania was on the way to record profits. Since Statler was not a money collector, but a money user, he *had* to build another hotel. His preoccupation was not with the question of whether or not to build, but where to build.

The acquiring of a Statler hotel had become such a status symbol and such good business that every major city in the country constantly courted him. He eliminated the West Coast cities, considering them too far away for effective personal supervision. The Mid-West, then, or New England? Chicago or Boston?

He made an inspection tour of both cities, talked to the local business and civic leaders, then returned home to announce his decision: the next Statler hotel would be built in — Buffalo!

All but his closest associates were amazed. He already

had a hotel in Buffalo, and surely the town wasn't large enough or prosperous enough to have two! The industrial index of both Boston and Chicago was far higher than Buffalo's. Then why in the world would he choose Buffalo? Again it was loyalty and pride.

Buffalo was where he had been given credit that saved his tottering restaurant, Buffalo where he had his first experience in hotel keeping at the Pan-American Exposition, Buffalo where he built his first modern hotel, Buffalo where his poker-playing cronies lived, and where he felt comfortable.

His existing hotel there was well maintained and prosperous, but obsolete by his present standards. "Buffalo deserves the most modern Statler ever built," he said. In other words, he wanted a monument to himself in his home town.

The location of the new structure was to be a five-sided plot at Niagara Square, bounded by Delaware Avenue and Mohawk, Franklin and Genesee Streets. Facing the square were the new buildings of the Civic Center development. To further improve the environment, Statler purchased land around the site, including a lot across the street where he planned to build a garage for those guests arriving by motor car. He foresaw that automobiles would one day replace the trains and he was going to be prepared.

To increase the area's traffic further he financed the construction of the Erlanger Theatre nearby. It was a legitimate theatre and would draw to the neighborhood Buffalo's literate and successful people. Statler explained the project this way: "Most people want to make a night of it when they go to the theatre. They eat out, either before or after the performance. And there we'll be with our restaurants right across the street."

There was one roadblock in his drive to make his new hotel the social center of Buffalo — it was the Iroquois Hotel. The Iroquois had a firm claim to society's loyalty, largely because of its suave and personable manager, Elmore C. Green. Statler reasoned that if Green had Buffalo society in his back pocket, the only thing to do was to hire Green away. This was not feasible, however, because Green was loyal to the old hotel.

A Buffalo newspaper columnist commented on Statler's problem: "It will take more than modern plumbing in every room to capture the gallivanting trade from the old Iroquois."

There was only one solution to the problem, and finally Statler embraced it. He purchased the Iroquois for $1,835,-412 and turned it into an office building. This was a ruthless use of money, of the power that money bestows upon a man, but no one complained much. Green was satisfied, he had a new job with Statler, managing the most luxurious hotel in the Mid-West. Perhaps there were a few nostalgic wails from Buffalo's elite, but after being forced into the Statler, they had to admit that it was really a better setting in which to display their gowns and jewels.

Having prudently dispatched the dangerous competition, Statler set out to barricade his fief against any future invasions. His new house was to contain 1,100 guestrooms which in itself was enough to discourage any other hotel from competing in the area. Statler wanted a little extra "insurance," however, and when the main structure began to rise he had the builder pour the foundation for a future wing of 500 rooms, to be completed "whenever Buffalo needs it."

Over the years a number of hotel men expressed interest in the Buffalo area, and each time this happened Statler held a press conference. When the reporters filed into his office they'd find him studying the old plans for the wing. And each time his statement was the same — the time was "just about right" for the addition of 500 medium-priced rooms.

The appearance of the story was always sufficiently

discouraging to the competition. Statler never did build the wing; he didn't have to. He once remarked, "That concrete foundation was the best investment I ever made."

The new Statler Hotel (the old one was renamed Hotel Buffalo) opened on May 19, 1923, and the Mayor proclaimed a civic holiday in honor of the event. There was the usual banquet for leading citizens and after it they danced to the imported music of Vincent Lopez and his Pennsylvania Hotel orchestra.

The *National Hotel Review* wrote:

> The hotel is an Arabian Night's Dream of the epitome of luxury and convenience brought to a fruitful realization. It will long stand as one of the most wonderful buildings for the entertainment of the traveling public that has ever been conjured up by the mind of man.

If that report seemed rather much, it was clearly topped by a bit of hyperbole composed by C. F. Marsh, a member of the English Department at the University of Buffalo:

> Thy lofty walls lift skyward in the mist;
> Sheer, straight and strong,
> Like cliffs by the Creator's hand, huge-carved;
> Thy courts like canyons.
> Thy majesty o'erlooks an inland sea.
> The morning sun gilds first thy battlements,
> At eventide last lingering looks on thee.
> But thy sheer walls were reared aloft by man;
> Man made thee for a purpose.
> Thou must serve.
> Let service match with excellence thy size!
> Be ample to the needs of all mankind —
> Vast temple to the ministry of man.

Whatever the literary merits of the poem, it was an indication that Statler had grown far beyond the level of mere commercial success — along with Edison and Ford he was becoming an American folk hero.

187

CHAPTER 27

"INDOOR GOLF"

As with all things in life, a business empire cannot stand still — it either grows or diminishes. Statler was determined that his organization would continue to grow, not just in numbers of buildings but in efficiency and quality of service to the public.

Every aspect of hotel work, from the duties of bus boy to manager, had been analyzed and formalized. In theory, the traveler checking into a Statler Hotel would receive perfect service. There was one flaw, however; the work had to be performed by human beings who were subject to fatigue and boredom and frustration and jealousy and hangover.

To combat these, Statler devised a thing he called "indoor golf." It was nothing more or less than frequent and unannounced inspections. The name came out of an experience he had at the Pennsylvania. One day he and Dunc McLeod planned a golf game and they left Statler's suite on the top floor and punched the elevator bell. By habit, Statler clicked a stopwatch. There was an unusually long wait for service that morning and when they were finally delivered to the lobby Statler clicked his watch again and frowned at it. John Woelfle was in charge of the elevator service and when he saw the frown on the boss's face he knew he was in for trouble.

Statler walked up to him and shook the stopwatch under his nose. "Do you know how long it took us to get service to the lobby?"

Woelfle made a tactical error: he gave an alibi. "This is a rush hour, Mr. Statler."

"Damn it, that is all the more reason to give good service. By God, I'll show you how it's done." He threw his golf clubs on the floor (they didn't make too much noise because he carried only three clubs — brassie, mashie and putter), stepped before the bank of elevators and took over the starter's job. There was an immediate and dramatic improvement in service.

After some ten minutes of this, Dunc McLeod became impatient and said, "Stat, we gonna play golf or not?"

Statler grinned at him. "I'm playing indoor golf, Dunc. It's almost as much fun."

When Statler set out on an inspection tour he took great precautions to keep the fact a secret but invariably there were leaks. The various managers tried to protect each other and frequently wired two little words: "He's coming."

On one of his first inspection visits to Cleveland, manager Russell Keith met him at the front entrance and said, "It's wonderful to have you here, Mr. Statler. Everything is in tiptop condition and I'm sure you're going to be pleased. We have a room all ready for you, here's the key."

Statler looked at the key as if it was about to bite him. "To hell with that," he said. Then he walked behind the desk and picked a key at random off the rack. "This is the room I'll take," he announced.

In the room that had not been prepared for him, he found a number of things wrong. He lay on the bed to look at the ceiling and discovered a stain. He said to the manager, "The guest's view of the room is often the ceiling. Keep it clean."

When he moved off the bed it squeaked. "Have the carpenter brace that bed with an iron bar through the spring," he ordered.

He inspected the supply of stationery in the desk,

the pins and needles and thread on the dresser, the cleanliness of the bathroom. From there he went to the public rooms, the kitchens, the basements. When he left after twenty-four hours, the staff's nerves were shot.

Month by month he took increasing precautions to conceal his movements from his managers, and he was frequently successful in making an unannounced arrival. Once, in St. Louis, he entered the elevator which, after various stops, arrived at the top floor. While waiting for the down signal, the operator turned to the slight, rather rumpled man in his car and said:

"Well, where did you want to get off?"

"Sixth floor," the passenger replied.

"Why didn't you say so?"

"You didn't ask me," he snapped. "Young man, your standard instructions are to ask, 'Floors, please.' And if you're in doubt about some passenger, say, 'Sir, what is your floor?' Study your instructions. I'm Mr. Statler."

Later, after Statler had gone, the operator said to the manager, "He didn't look like Mr. Statler."

"He was," said the manager with a heavy sigh. "Believe me, he was."

Upon entering the dining room in the Detroit house, he was attended at once by a captain. "I don't want you to wait on me. I want the regular waiter for this station. If he's not good enough to give me the proper service, he's not good enough for our guests."

Another time Statler and a friend came down to breakfast before leaving for a game of golf. There was a house rule that guests in the main dining room had to wear jackets and ties. Statler and his friend were dressed in plus-fours and sweaters.

"I'm sorry, gentlemen," the head waiter said, "but you'll have to go back and get your jackets and ties before I can let you in here."

Statler didn't say a word, didn't identify himself, but

turned around and did as directed. That evening, however, he said to the manager, "Give that captain a raise. He's on the job."

H. William Klare was manager of the Detroit house, and one of the bright young men of the organization whom (along with H. B. Callis and Bert Stanbro) Statler was grooming for corporate leadership. One morning Klare summoned Frank Duggan, his assistant manager, and said, "Cleveland has tipped me off that the old man is on his way here for some indoor golf. I want you to shake down this house from top to bottom. Check every bed, every faucet, every frypan. Let's not let him find a damn thing."

Duggan called all the department heads together and gave them their marching orders. For the next six hours there was an orgy of cleaning, straightening, brushing, polishing, sweeping, scrubbing, until the place literally glittered. During his own final inspection Duggan came upon a pantry door that was loose on its hinges.

"Just close that damn door and lock it," Duggan directed.

Statler arrived a short time later and began his tour with Bill Klare, Duggan and a secretary in his wake. He started at the top floor and worked down until at last he was in the kitchen. He checked the tops of the stoves for grease, the tops of the refrigerators for dust. There was none. Passing down a hall toward the food storage bins he glanced at the locked closet door. There was absolutely no objective reason for him to do so; the door was small and inconspicuous and obviously led to nowhere but some instinct, some intuition, some extrasensory perception made him stop.

"What's in there?" he asked.

"Mops," Duggan said. "Just mops, Mr. Statler."

Statler tried the door and found it locked. "Must be very valuable mops," he said. "Give me the key."

Statler unlocked the door and pulled on its handle

whereupon the door came completely off its hinges and fell clattering to the floor, striking Statler a slight glancing blow on his head as it went.

Statler put a handkerchief to his head and said, with deceptive mildness, "Poor maintenance, Klare. Poor maintenance."

Salesmanship, the house organ, was extensively used by Statler to launch a campaign against "disinterested service." He didn't want his people merely to go through the motions, but to be genuinely interested in each guest. He published guests' letters of complaint, and added his own comments:

I am going to quote from three or four of the letters. Just read these over carefully and note particularly that *disinterested service* was the cause of these complaints. *Disinterested service* is at the bottom of most of our troubles. Here's one that came in today:

"My friends have complained to me that when they phone this hotel they are told by your operators that we do not respond. I have told a clerk at the desk and the telephone operators about these complaints, but *they do not seem to pay any attention to me.*"

Here's another:

"It took me from nine to twelve o'clock to get a porter to my room. I called about every fifteen minutes and each time talked with a man at the porter's desk. When a porter finally did come in I asked him, 'Are you busy tonight?' He answered, 'No, I have not done anything for three hours.' On each occasion when I talked with the porter's desk, I was answered with the statement somewhat as follows: 'I'll get a man there soon as I can.' That was all the result that I got."

And here's another:

"On Thursday night my wife and I arrived in – –, deciding we would like to stop at your hotel because of its reputation for excellent service. Upon making inquiry of a very dapper room clerk at the registry window, I was informed in very short, almost brusque, manner that there were no rooms to be had. He did not even allow me to approach him again to make further inquiries as to a nearby hotel, but went about his work as if I were imposing on his valued time. We left, found a neat room in a nearby hotel, and received courtesy and plenty of it on every hand from every employee. We are now, of course, timid to even recommend your hotel to our traveling friends."

How each of these complaints might have been prevented is obvious to you as it is to me. And yet, as simple as it was in each case to have been courteous and attentive to these people, someone failed to measure up and to make good.

There are remedies for such troubles. Here is one: *Listen carefully to what is asked of you, and then go out of YOUR WAY, if necessary to be helpful. Try hard to give a patron the same attention that you would want to be shown if you were in his place.*

It is a simple rule, but it is so important that no person, no hotel can succeed unless it is observed.

Soft spots in the organization were spotted by Statler, not only through letters, not only from indoor golf, but from the bookkeeping. It was thus that he discovered trouble in the Pennsylvania's tearoom. This room was important because it was a pilot Statler was using in an effort to prove that prohibition did not mean the end of public room profits.

The entire hotel industry was frightened when prohibition became law, for the barrooms accounted for a fair share of every hotel's net profits. Statler decried the gloom, saying that the groundfloor space occupied by the bars could still be made to show some profit by installing attractive tearooms for the ladies. He proved the thesis in his own hotels, particularly in the Pennsylvania. Ladies who came to Herald Square to shop at Macy's or

Gimbels or Saks made a point of having lunch or afternoon tea at the Pennsylvania. It became *the* thing to do.

The tearoom deserved new and more feminine decor, Statler decided, and told Rorimer to "give it the works." The result was a gay and glittering room with crystal chandeliers, deep carpets, and pillars and paintings and pottery, all imported from Europe. What a perfect setting for a lady's tea!

The room reopened with a great deal of excitement and extravagant compliments. Then by the end of the month, business had fallen off by a quarter, and by the end of the second month by a half.

"What's the matter with the tearoom?" Statler snapped at his manager.

"I don't know," was the puzzled reply.

"Well, find out!"

During the following week there was a crash program of research. Assistant managers in striped pants stood around with stopwatches to time the service. The head chef personally monitored each plate of food as it left the kitchens. The executive housekeeper inspected rugs and ledges for dust. The carpenter examined every chair to see if it was solid and comfortable.

"All right," Statler said to the manager at the end of the week, "what's wrong?"

"Mr. Statler, I can't find anything wrong," replied the unhappy manager.

"You can't?" he cried. "Well, by God, I can!" He grabbed up a sheaf of papers covered with figures. "We're losing money on that room. That's what in hell is wrong."

He began to pace his office, looking defiantly toward Alice Seidler a couple of times. He had cursed and he meant to curse and he dared her to object. She didn't. She kept her eyes cast discreetly downward on her work, appearing to have heard nothing.

"Call all the waitresses together for a meeting tomorrow morning at ten o'clock," Statler barked. "I want to hear what they have to say."

The next morning he was all charm and consideration. He looked over the gathering of twenty-five women with an avuncular smile, then said, "Ladies, we have a problem and I need your help. As you know, the patronage of our tearoom has fallen off and I just don't know why. One thing I do know, it's *not* the service. You ladies are courteous and efficient and I'm real proud of you, every one of you. I'm also convinced it's not the food. But it's *something*. Do you have any ideas?"

There was a pause, then a plump, motherly waitress stood up and said, "I think it's the new lights, Mr. Statler. They're too bright."

"Too bright?" Statler repeated as he looked up at the imported chandeliers.

"Yes, sir. They show up all the age lines in a woman's face, and all the makeup. I think that's why a lot of them have stopped coming here."

That day Statler had tent cards printed and placed on each table in the tearoom. They contained a questionnaire for the patrons, and asked if the lights should be brighter, just as they were, or dimmer. The response was 96 percent "dimmer."

It cost $15,000 to tear out the lighting and replace it with softer and more soothing illumination; but it was worth it. Once the ladies discovered they could again have tea without a public declaration of age, they returned in great numbers.

The tearoom experience only confirmed, in Statler's mind, the correctness of his slogan, "The Guest Is Always Right." He pushed it in his consumer advertising, then he turned to his employees and said, in *Salesmanship*:

> See what I have promised the public? Now it is up to you to make good on my promise. *Every* complaint from a guest *must* be satisfied to his *complete satisfaction*. If you

cannot solve the problem, take it to your superior. If he cannot solve it, he must take it to his superior. If necessary, the problem should come right on up to me. If it does, you may be sure *I'll* solve it.

Statler did not mean that every guest complaint would be justified or even reasonable; he meant that it was good business to meet the demands, however frivolous. It was a burden on his people, for no man enjoys being taken advantage of, and this was bound to happen from time to time.

A salesman stopping at the Cleveland house showed the room maid a freshly laundered shirt with a tear in it. He said the hotel laundry was responsible for the tear and he should be compensated. She reported this to the executive housekeeper. When the housekeeper examined the shirt she discovered that the shirt was an old one and the tear was a place where the threads had simply disintegrated. She pointed this out to the man, but with no success. He still demanded compensation. She took the problem to Eugene Kelly, the assistant manager.

"He has no legitimate claim," she said, "and *I'll* not approve it."

Kelly sighed and said, "Give me the shirt and I'll take it down to the laundry and see what they have to say."

The superintendent of the laundry took one look at the shirt and said, "We didn't even launder that shirt. It was done on the outside." He tossed the garment contemptuously back to Kelly.

"How can you be sure of that?" Kelly demanded.

"See that black wooden collar button holding the collar together? We don't use them. That shirt was done by Whiteside Laundry."

Minutes later Kelly walked into the office of Russell Keith, the hotel manager, dropped the shirt on his desk and told the story.

"Good!" Keith exclaimed. "Just leave that shirt right here. The old man is coming in tomorrow and we'll show him what we're up against."

Kelly was summoned to the manager's office the next morning to face Statler. "Tell Mr. Statler the story of the shirt," the manager said.

Statler listened to the end, his face impassive. "Well, now, Mr. Keith," Statler said to his manager at the completion of the story, "I'd like you to tell me how much you think your time is worth. And Kelly's time here. And the laundry superintendent's time. And the housekeeper's time. And the room maid's time. You don't have a ready figure? Well, would you say that it was worth more than five dollars? Oh, you would?" He slapped the desk sharply with his hand. "Then, why in hell's name didn't you pay the claim and get on with your work?"

Not all of Statler's corporate officers were in agreement with "the guest is always right" policy. They feared that it would seriously drain funds that should be dividends to the stockholders. To rebut this, Statler instructed Stoner to draw up a twelve-month report on funds disbursed in guest claims. The total turned out to be but a fraction of one percent of the net profits.

Not only was the cost infinitesimal, but the policy had resulted in nationwide publicity that could not have been purchased at any price.

Statler's single-minded, sometimes cantankerous insistence on service ultimately made his hotels a tourist attraction in themselves. Thousands of families traveled to Buffalo or Cleveland or St. Louis or Detroit or New York for the experience of staying in a Statler Hotel. They wrote Statler letters of praise and thanks, and in these letters he found the reward of a lifetime of labor.

One such public accolade came from Emily Post, who wrote in her newspaper column:

E. M. STATLER

We went to the Statler, a commercial hotel but most comfortable, with a much-advertised and really quite faultless service . . . The food at the Statler Hotel was so extraordinarily good that I asked where the maitre d'hotel and his chefs had come from. I thought that possibly on account of the war they had secured the staff of Henri's or Voisin's or Paillard's in Paris, and was really surprised to hear the head chef was from Chicago and the maitre d'hotel from New York. The dining room service was quite as extraordinarily good as the food. We did not wait more than a moment before they brought the first course and as soon as we had finished that our plates were whisked away and the second put before us. Never, even in Paris, have we had a better or more perfectly cooked chicken casserole . . . Our waiter brought in crisp, fresh salad, and expertly and quickly made his own dressing. He was, in fact, a prince of his kind, serving all our meals without that everlasting patting and fussing and fixing that most waiters do until what you have ordered is so shopworn and handled and cold that it is not fit to eat.

This was reprinted in *Salesmanship*, under the headline WE'RE PROUD OF THIS ONE. Statler always shared the good and the bad with his employees, and this was one reason he was able to create in his sprawling empire a feeling of family loyalty and pride.

CHAPTER 28

THE GRAND TOUR

Statler once believed in omens and portents. When he was a boy working in the McLure House in Wheeling he paid a traveling phrenologist for a private character reading. The "Professor," after examining his skull, gave him a written report that found, in part:

> You are not at all brilliant . . . show off to poor advantage . . . You will pass along through life without being especially noted for anything . . . could do passably well at storekeeping, only you would be too loath to venture . . . You should get your living from something sure, for you could not dare to run any risk . . .

For a number of years the boy carried those words in his pocket so that he could conveniently refer to them. He believed that they told the truth about his character but he set out to change himself. By the time the torn and tattered paper disintegrated, he had, to his own satisfaction, altered his character to conform to his ambition.

As an adult he lost all interest in the occult. Even when his Pennsylvania Hotel band leader, Vincent Lopez, began to make remarkably accurate forecasts through the use of numerology, he displayed only a passing curiosity. He had made of his life exactly what he had planned, he had done it through hard work. He had defied the gods . . . or at least the bumps on his head.

It was, therefore, with no misgivings at all one morning that he said to Alice Seidler, "It's time to build a hotel in Boston."

That was all he needed to say for he knew she would set the wheels in motion. She would notify McKowne, Stoner, Hennessy and Newton that the boss was ready for Boston. She would begin correspondence with contractors and suppliers, inviting bids on the thousand-odd items that make a hotel. And during the hectic, tension-filled days ahead she would be a sort of traffic manager, monitoring the flow of men and ideas across Statler's desk.

The "Big Four" of the company also depended upon her, mainly to keep them informed of Statler's moods and attitudes. Several times a week one or another officer of the company would show her a memo and say, "Do you think I should take this up with E. M. this morning?"

Her advice was invariably followed, for she knew more about Statler's moods and motivations than anyone else in the company. She was more than a secretary, she was an assistant, an associate from whom he kept nothing. Surprisingly, there was no jealousy of her by the other executives. Or perhaps not so surprisingly, for she was a threat to no one. She remained soft-spoken and modest, she had no ambition beyond her present job, and she did not toady to Statler. When he asked her opinion she gave it to him straight, no matter how distasteful he might find it.

Alice Seidler did not intrigue, did not play palace politics, and so all men came freely and safely to her with their problems. And the one who came most frequently was Statler himself.

During the spring of 1926 the leaders of the American Hotel Association were organizing a European grand tour but Statler made no plans to join them until his secretary finally raised the question.

"I think you should go to Europe, Mr. Statler," she said one morning.

He sent a quick look across the office. "You think the

European hotels are better than mine? You think I could learn something over there?"

She shook her head. "I don't think you should go there to learn, but to forget, to have some fun. And, after all, you'd be surrounded by your friends."

"Humph!" Statler said, dismissing the subject.

The seed had been planted in his mind, which was all that she intended. There would likely follow a slow period of germination, *if* it was left alone. On the other hand, if it was fussed over, cultivated, force-fed, Statler would, in pique, pull it out by the roots and throw it away. He was always open to new ideas if they related to the hotel business, but extremely wary of any projects that bore the label, "for your own good."

Behind Alice Seidler's maneuver was the knowledge that he would never take such a trip alone. He would feel awkward and uncomfortable in the presence of the worldly and sophisticated Europeans — he would be unable to manufacture the small talk necessary to ease contact with strangers. However, surrounded by his own kind from the AHA, he would be sure to find the trip fun and relaxing. Or at least, this was how Alice Seidler figured it.

And she figured it right. He joined the party.

Two hundred and fifty hotel men and their wives signed up for the trip and booked passage on the S. S. *La France* scheduled to sail out of New York harbor on April 3, 1926. John Bowman, president of the Biltmore Hotels chain, gave a bon voyage party in the Commodore ballroom on the evening of April 2. He went to great lengths and much expense to reproduce the French Line's North River pier 56. The press report the next day read:

> Mr. Bowman outdid all his previous efforts to provide novel entertainment for his guests. On leaving the elevators, the guests passed through a door and found themselves on the pier in the real atmosphere of such places when a great liner sails. Trunks and baggage of all kinds were piled in

heaps on the floor. Stevedores were busily engaged in loading supplies by means of huge winches . . . and the noise of whistles and sirens all helped to create the illusion that the ship was about to sail . . .

The next day at sailing time, Statler had George Olsen's Hotel Pennsylvania band down at the pier to play gay music as the *La France* edged out into the channel. Statler and his son Milton stood at the ship's rail to wave goodbye to the Big Four, McKowne, Stoner, Hennessy and Newton.

By the time the ship had cleared the Narrows and headed into the Atlantic it was clear who was going to be the life of the party — E. M. Statler! He danced tirelessly with all the wives, played poker tenaciously with the husbands. "Well, what are we here for?" was his cry as he led them into rounds of shipboard play. He acted as if the whole excursion was his, that he was the host; he paid the bar tabs, sent flowers and candy to the staterooms. He made the trip memorable for everyone.

When the party docked in London they were greeted by representatives of the British Hotel Association and escorted to their hotel quarters. Late that afternoon Tom Green, president of the AHA, came into Statler's room and reported:

"The Duke of York (*) and a committee from Parliament is receiving our officers tomorrow morning and the Duke has specifically requested that you be present."

"Why?" Statler asked.

"He wants to meet you. Hell, Stat, you're famous."

"I am? Way over here?"

Tom Green smiled at his old friend. "Yep. The Duke wants to meet a fourteen-karat, gold-plated, Yankee hotel millionaire genius."

(*) The Duke of York became King George VI and led Britain through World War II.

Statler shook his head in dismay. "I won't know what to say to him."

"You don't have to say anything. Make him do the talking. He doesn't own any hotels."

The Duke had a slight stammer which served to put Statler at ease, and the two of them had an extended talk, mostly about hotel plumbing.

The scene repeated itself throughout the tour. In Italy he was received by Pope Pius XI. Mussolini agreed to receive a delegation of the American hotel men only on the condition that he meet Statler. In Germany President von Hindenburg summoned Statler for lunch. He was received by the King of Belgium, and the Queen of the Netherlands. Every place he went there were demands that he make a speech, and he put one together. It hit exactly the right tone for the European audiences: he spoke of his pride at being a hotel man, because hotels throughout the world were cosmopolitan centers where foreigners could meet each other and learn about each other and discard the prejudices of which wars were made. His words were, of course, overly optimistic, but they had substance.

The French were so delighted with him that later (July 7, 1926) he was made a Chevalier in the Legion of Honor. On that occasion, French diplomat Dr. Marcel Knecht made the presentation, with the words ". . . (You are) a man who is loved by the men and women of the world. We pay tribute to you as a builder of the American hotel industry, as a man of magnetic personality, and as one who is unselfish in his patriotism and civic devotion. It (the decoration) is a just reward for a great service you have rendered to mankind. . ."

What had started out as a rather routine junket of a trade association turned into a triumphal tour for Statler. It soon began to pall on him, however. He had seen all the castles he wanted to see, had looked at paintings and statues until his senses could absorb no more. He was homesick.

As generous as Europe had been to him, he could work up no continuing enthusiasm for it. It was a civilization completed, offering no challenge to his particular talents. He longed for the younger, more fluid America. He wanted to build, to help shape the skylines of the cities, not just to sit back and admire what other men had done hundreds of years ago.

His impatience finally led him to make an uncharitable remark to his friend, Tom Green: "We can't learn anything from these European hotels. Let's go home."

The executive offices in the Pennsylvania Hotel were braced for his return. They all knew from experience that the longer Statler was away from work, the higher his velocity upon his return. This time there was apt to be a gale force sweeping through the offices.

The feelings of the staff were not entirely apprehension; there was speculation and curiosity about a certain widow who had been on the European tour. Gossip had come back that she had set her cap for Statler and was doing rather well. Everyone was eager to see what she looked like and to judge the relationship. There was not a long wait.

Within a week after his return to New York, Statler held a dinner party at which the widow was to be guest of honor. "Ah!" everyone said, "he is going to announce their engagement!"

No one ever found out if that was Statler's intention, for the widow had the misfortune to get very drunk that night. Statler took her home early and saw her very seldom afterwards.

CHAPTER 29

FAMILY INTERMEDIARY

Europe had worked a change in Statler — he became quite social. He had previously confined his entertaining to his own kind, to hotel men, but now he had enough security to swim in larger pools. New York leaders of finance, of the arts, of politics became his guests, and he theirs. Mayor Jimmy Walker became a buddy.

He did not dress any better, his language was salty as ever, he claimed no special skills or knowledge outside the hotel business, and despite the booming stock market that made men rich overnight (on paper!) he clung to the old-fashioned American dream that the only way to success was by hard work, thrift, and service to others. He pointed to himself as proof: "If I can make it with my education and my handicaps, then any American can make it, *if* he works as hard as I have."

He had not altered himself in any way, he merely exposed himself to an ever widening circle of people who found him to be a completely engaging man.

At one of his dinner parties a guest had to make a last-minute cancellation because of death in the family. Statler heard the news over the phone, replaced the receiver and looked across the office at his secretary.

"Miss Seidler, I'm having a small dinner Saturday night and one of the invited guests can't make it. Would you fill in?"

"Oh, I'm sorry, Mr. Statler, but I can't."

"You . . . can't?"

"No, sir. I have an engagement for Saturday. You know Mr. Kauffman from Chicago?"

Statler's expression was one of quizzical amazement. A date? Miss Seidler had a date? It had never occurred to him that she had a life outside this office. Though he knew it was unjust, he could not entirely rid himself of the feeling that she was being somehow disloyal to the organization. He returned his eyes to the work in front of him and for the rest of the day was very grumpy. The following day he began a campaign to involve her with his children and himself. The result was a limited success which, in his eyes, was no success at all.

As Christmas approached he said, "Miss Seidler, I've made plans to take the children to Lake Saranac for the holidays. I find now I have to be in Chicago until about the twentieth of December. Will you take them on ahead and get settled in the Lodge? I'll join you all in time for Christmas."

"I'll take them on ahead, Mr. Statler, but I won't be able to stay for Christmas. I always spend it with my own family."

A dark frown wrinkled his face.

She refused to be intimidated. "It's not right of you to ask an employee to give up Christmas with his family unless there is an emergency. This is no emergency."

"All right! All right!" he said, waving his hand to end the conversation. He couldn't resist the final two words: "Hell's fire!"

Another problem intruded on the following week. Statler was reading the morning mail when he came across a bill from a Long Island shipyard. His son Milton had placed an order for a 40-foot ketch and the builder was prudently asking the father's approval. Statler threw the letter angrily on the desk and barked:

"Miss Seidler, I want you to tell Milton that I'm not buying him another boat until he straightens out and acts the way he should."

"Why don't you tell him, Mr. Statler?"

"I can't. I'm not speaking to him."

"But you should be. That's part of the trouble. . ."

"I know, I know!" he said with some annoyance. After a moment of silence he said, quite humbly, "I'm not a very good father, I know that. I try to be, but something always seems to go wrong between us. I . . . I need your help."

What woman could resist such a plea?

The role of family intermediary was forced on Alice Seidler, not only by the father but also the children. They had few inhibitions with her, for they knew she would tell their father what should be told and withhold what should be withheld. She was, in brief, something they had never really had — a mother symbol.

"I think you should try and pay more attention to Marian," Alice Seidler said to Statler one day. "She needs very much to know that you love her."

"She doesn't know that?" he asked in surprise.

"Well, she's in the middle of adolescence and she's not quite sure of anything. She keeps asking me who her real mother was, and why she gave her out for adoption. She's afraid her mother was a bad woman."

"I don't know who she was, and I don't know of any way to find out."

"So I guessed."

"What did you say to her?"

"I said simply that I knew nothing about her mother but I was convinced she must have been a very fine woman, otherwise Marian wouldn't be such a fine girl."

"Exactly!" Statler exclaimed. "But I should never have been able to say those words."

"You don't have to say anything, Mr. Statler. Just put your arms around her every now and then."

"I'll try."

CHAPTER 30

CORNELL UNIVERSITY IN 1925

Shortly after his return from Europe in the spring of 1927 Statler received an invitation to attend the first commencement ceremonies of the struggling School of Hotel Administration at Cornell University. He rejected it in a blunt letter to the dean of the school, Howard Meek. This was not the end of it, however, for supporters of the school began some flanking attacks. First, there was a gambit by David Newton who, during a meeting of the Executive Board, casually said:

"E. M., I think we can get a lot of good publicity when you go to the Cornell graduation."

"There's good publicity and bad publicity," Statler snapped. "If I went to that shindig, it would be bad publicity because it would be dishonest."

"Dishonest?"

"I don't approve of that school, damn it!"

Newton feigned surprise. "When the AHA pledged funds to start the school, and then couldn't meet the bill, weren't you the one who raised the money?"

"Don't give me that, Dave. You know perfectly well I couldn't let the Association become a deadbeat. I did it to save our reputation, not for the school. Now, that's the end of it."

Not quite, it wasn't. Two days later Statler received a long distance call from Leon Rothschild, owner of the Rothschild store in Ithaca, and a close personal friend.

"E. M., I want you to do me a favor."

MRS. ELLSWORTH M. STATLER

This portrait of Mrs. Alice Seidler Statler was made on her eightieth birthday. The terms of Mr. Statler's will established the Statler Foundation to further the education of young people for the hotel industry. Mrs. Statler, who became chairman of the Statler Foundation, serves as the principal executive officer.

STATLER HALL IS THE HOME OF CORNELL'S
FAMOUS SCHOOL OF HOTEL ADMINISTRATION.

Major beneficiary of the Statler Foundation is the School
of Hotel Administration at Cornell University, which Mr.
Statler visited in 1925 and found to meet his high standards
for education in hotel management. Statler Hall, shown in
two pictures above, is built in three sections: a 36-room inn
and the Statler Club for the university's faculty, which
provide an operating laboratory for the School; the central
classroom section that houses classrooms, laboratories, and
offices; and the Alice Statler Auditorium which holds additional classrooms, laboratories and the School's library.
Grants for building, maintenance, research, scholarships,
and other educational projects brought the total sum given
to the School to over $7,500,000 in 1966.

Mrs. Ellsworth M. Statler enters the door of Statler Inn to attend the 38th annual Hotel Ezra Cornell, an event her husband first attended in 1925. Her entrance marks the opening of a series of receptions, dinners, lectures, and exhibits — all planned for guests invited from the hotel and restaurant industry.

SAN FRANCISCO

The Statler Wing of the City College of San Francisco houses this college's program in hotel and restaurant management. The Statler Foundation contributed $125,000 for the construction of this wing.

NEW YORK CITY

The Statler Wing of the New York City Community College is the home of its hotel and restaurant management department. The Statler Foundation contributed $150,000 to build this wing.

"Anything, you know that, Leon."

"I want you to bring your golf clubs up here to Ithaca on the fifteenth of the month and let me lick you. . ."

"One dollar a hole says you can't."

". . . and the next day we can go to the commencement of the Hotel School at Cornell."

"Oh, now, Leon. . ." Statler wailed.

"A personal favor."

"Damn it to hell!"

There was no bite in the words, however. Statler sounded like a man who had been had, and knew it.

There was a reason why Leon Rothschild was perhaps the only man in the country who could make such a demand on Statler; he and his uncle had once saved Statler from failure. The Rothschilds had the franchise for Syracuse Pottery and when Statler opened his Ellicott Square restaurant in Buffalo they were the low bidders and supplied him with his china.

When the restaurant tottered on the verge of bankruptcy, it was the Rothschilds (uncle Dan and nephew Leon) who announced their faith in the young man from Wheeling and extended limitless credit. As the largest single creditor, their action influenced all the other purveyors and Statler was saved. The gratitude and loyalty Statler felt for the Rothschilds was undiminished over the years and he refused to buy his china from any other firm. Not that he didn't continue to bargain fiercely with them on price.

Old Uncle Dan Rothschild was sitting in the lobby of the Cleveland Statler one afternoon when another purveyor sat down beside him and opened a conversation.

"Ever sell E. M. Statler?" the purveyor asked.

"Yep," Uncle Dan replied.

"Ever make a dime?"

"Nope. Made a nickel."

Now, after almost thirty years of close association,

Rothschild was asking his first personal favor. He said on the phone, "Let me tell you what these college kids are doing. They are going to cater and serve a banquet just as if it was a hotel opening. They are naming it the Ezra Cornell Hotel, after the founder of the University, and they are inviting all the hotel men to be their guests and observe what they have learned. Now, how would those kids feel if you, the biggest man in the business, didn't show up? It would be a terrible blow."

"All right, Leon, I'll come. But, damn it, I'm not happy about it."

As the train pulled into the Ithaca station, Statler stepped down on the platform to be met by a welcoming committee from the University, several newspaper reporters, and Leon Rothschild.

"The reporters want a statement from you about the hotel school," Rothschild whispered in Statler's ear. "If you can't say something good about it, just don't make any statement at all."

After giving his friend a reproachful look, Statler turned to the reporters and said he would have no statement to make "at this time."

A young man stepped out of the crowd, extended his hand to Statler and said, "Welcome to Cornell, Mr. Statler. I'm Victor Grohmann, your student guide."

Statler took the young man's hand with all the enthusiasm one feels in the presence of a communicable disease. Dean Meek had assigned a student guide to each of the hotel men coming for the banquet, and Victor Grohmann(*) had been given the most difficult and important man of all. He was going to need every ounce of his own patience and composure before the day was over.

(*) Some years later Grohmann established his own advertising firm of Needham & Grohmann which became one of the outstanding agencies specializing in hotel, resort and travel advertising.

"I thought, sir, that you might like to sit in on some of our classes this afternoon," the young man said.

"What happened to our golf game?" Statler demanded of Rothschild.

"First things first," his friend grinned.

When Professor Frank Randolph convened his class on stationary engineering and boiler firing that afternoon he faced not only his regular students but a half-dozen hotel men including the formidable E. M. Statler. Randolph knew how important it was for the school to win these men's approval and support. The emergency funds raised by the AHA were about exhausted and if the hotel industry did not sponsor a drive for endowments, the school was unlikely to survive.

With care and precision the professor launched into a discussion of the engineering problems of heating a hotel with a coal-fired boiler. As he continued his language became more and more scientific and he referred several times to the British measurements of thermal units. His students may well have understood what he was talking about, but it was far over the heads of his visitors.

After forty minutes he ended his lecture and made a graceful little speech of welcome to the visitors. He wondered if any of them would like to say anything to the students. Perhaps Mr. Statler had a few words?

Statler stood up and the young, eager faces all turned to him. He said, "Boys, you're wasting your time here. You don't have to learn this stuff to be a hotel man. When I have an engineering problem I hire an engineer. I don't know a damn thing about the British thermal units, and there's no reason for you to, either. Go on home and get a job."

There was a moment of stunned silence. Statler jammed his old hat on his head and walked out of the room, hurriedly followed by Rothschild and young Grohmann. As the three men moved across the campus there was an awkward silence. Grohmann finally broke it. "Dean Meek would be pleased to have you for lunch, sir. That is, if you have the time."

Ignoring him, Statler turned to Rothschild and said petulantly, "Damn it, Leon, I told the truth in there."

Rothschild gave a slight shrug. "Ah, the truth. It is often different things to different people."

"British thermal units will never be anything but hogwash to me."

"I understand that the boys are taught some other subjects."

It was a gentle rebuke, but a clear one. Statler knew he had been guilty of bad manners, and also would be accused of prejudging the entire school. He felt a twinge of guilt, an emotion that he seldom experienced, and he didn't like it one bit.

"Son," he said abruptly to Grohmann, "forget about the lunch. Let's get on with the inspection tour. I want to see everything you have, I want to observe every class."

"Yes, sir!" the young man grinned.

Since the Hotel School had no buildings or facilities if its own, it had to take the University's left-over space scattered throughout the campus. For the next two days Statler could be seen hustling from one end of the campus to the other to look in on classes in hotel bookkeeping, food control, housekeeping, maintenance, purchasing, and all the other aspects of hotel operation.

The two days closed with the great banquet prepared and served by the senior class. Statler, who was scheduled to speak, sat on the dais beside Dean Meek. A number of elaborate and delicious courses were served while the guests studied Statler's face, not only for his opinion of the meal, but seeking a clue to the words he would soon speak.

At last the meal was ended, the student chefs were

called out of the kitchen and presented to the applauding diners, and it was time for Statler's address.

He was introduced by Meek, and slowly came to his feet. There was a silence in the hall that could only be described as apprehensive. Statler frowned, seemed to search for the proper opening words. He found them. The entire speech was two sentences long:

"I'm converted. Meek can have any damn thing he wants."

CHAPTER 31

THE BOSTON STATLER

It was against everyone's advice that Statler went into Boston to build a hotel in 1927. It was even against his own advice. Over the past decade there had been a nationwide hotel building boom which he viewed with some alarm. The time would come, he warned the industry, when there would be more beds than travelers to fill them. His words were prophetic: after the market crash in 1929, occupancy in most hotels dropped to 50 percent or less. During the following years four out of five hotels went into bankruptcy; three large hotel chains were wiped out.

Foreseeing the crisis, Statler still went into Boston, though not without misgivings, and certainly not without the most careful planning. For nine years he had watched the development of the Back Bay area and in May 1922 he had purchased a triangular-shaped plot containing 60,000 square feet and costing $450,000. He had plans drawn and redrawn time and again. As each set of plans reached his desk he'd study them and then throw them angrily aside. "That's the way we did it in Detroit. Don't we have any fresh ideas?" He would not believe that the perfect hotel, the most profitable hotel, had already been built.

The nay-sayers on his staff warned him that Boston was a cheap town and his better rooms would never be filled. Admittedly there was wealth and society in Boston, there were the Brahmans, but he would never win them away from the elegant Copley Plaza.

These facts were stubborn and could not be blinked away, but instead of discouraging Statler they only served to raise his fighting spirit and he took them on, one at a time.

To his architect he said, "Draw up new plans with an additional three hundred inexpensive rooms."

"Do you want to reduce the number of suites, Mr. Statler?" the architect asked.

"Hell's fire, no! I'll get enough of the Copley trade to fill them."

"Something's got to give."

"Not at all. Just add two more stories."

This was done only then to discover that the Massachusetts building code limited all structures to the height of 125 feet. The proposed Statler Hotel, with the two extra stories, was 155 feet high.

"Miss Seidler, get Mayor Curley of Boston on the phone," Statler ordered. James Curley was a personal friend of Statler as well as a leading advocate of a Statler Hotel in his town. When he was finally on the line, Statler came directly to the point.

"Mister Mayor, you got a building code that limits buildings to 125 feet high. I need 155 feet. Can you get that approved for me? . . . I know it's a state ordinance, not a city one, but you run the state, don't you? . . . Don't be modest, damn it . . . either you give me 155 feet or I don't come into Boston."

Mayor Curley had no difficulty with the legislature, and Statler was given his 155 feet. Even with this victory behind him, he was hesitant, an attitude quite unlike him. He was waiting for something, and he didn't know exactly what it was. There was some instinct working within him, telling him there was something more to be done to protect his investment. He had too much respect for his own intuition and hunches to ignore this feeling. He had delayed building for nine years; he could wait a few more months.

The elusive idea suddenly crystalized during one of his wakeful nights and he grabbed the phone to call McKowne. The idea was so simple that it took a certain kind of genius to think of it.

"McKowne!" he shouted into the phone, "I've solved our Boston problem."

"Oh?" came the sleepy voice carrying a touch of weary patience.

"We'll incorporate an office building into the hotel. We'll make it the smartest office building in town, a prestige address. It will not only bring added business to our dining rooms, but the rentals will support the hotel if we hit some bad times."

Back to the drawing board went the plans. This time there emerged a massive structure of 14 stories covering 80,000 square feet of land. The lower floors were faced with terra cotta, and the upper ones were of brick with terra cotta trim. The part devoted to offices occupied about one quarter of the site and contained interior corridors connecting to the hotel which contained 1,300 guestrooms. The lowest construction bid came to $14 million, and this figure was to be increased as Statler kept adding innovations.

Just before ground breaking in the fall of 1926 Statler called a meeting of his Board of Directors. The Board was composed of estimable men but powerless. Statler owned the majority of the stock and he treated his Board with affection and condescension. He delighted in shocking them.

On the morning of this meeting Alice Seidler noticed that he walked around the offices with a little boy grin of mischief on his face.

"We're going to have a very interesting Board meeting this afternoon, Miss Seidler," he said just before lunch.

"Yes, I could tell you have something up your sleeve."

"You could?" He was surprised; he always considered himself inscrutable.

THE BOSTON STATLER

"You shouldn't tease your board, Mr. Statler," Alice Seidler said gently.

He laughed. "I've got a great idea, the best in years, and it's going to shake up a few of the old fuddy-duddies."

The afternoon meeting was conducted by Statler with great decorum. When the agenda was finished and the Board about to leave, he said casually, "I've decided to put a radio in every room of the Boston house."

There was a moment of stunned silence.

"Western Electric is designing us a master receiver and the architect is working on the room installation. Beside each bed will be a night table with a drawer that holds two sets of earphones and a switch that allows the guest to choose one of two different broadcasting channels."

"How much will this cost?" one of the directors asked after he had recovered his voice.

"Fifty thousand dollars."

"Good lord, E. M., that's as much as last year's net from the St. Louis house."

Statler considered that observation irrelevant, unworthy of comment. He said, "Radio is the greatest entertainment medium yet invented. Soon every home in the nation will have a radio receiving set. Now, our advertising has always claimed that a Statler room contains all the comforts of home." He gave a pixy grin. "You gentlemen wouldn't have us run dishonest advertising, would you?"

Again his words were prophetic. Radio listening became a national craze. Theatre and motion picture box office receipts declined as people stayed home to listen to their favorite programs. A whole new galaxy of stars was born: Rudy Vallee, Ben Bernie, Billy Jones and Ernie Hare (the Happiness Boys), Jack Pearl ("Voss you dere, Sharlie?"), Joe Penner ("Wanna buy a duck?"), and probably the most spectacularly successful comedy act of the century, Amos and Andy. Charles Correll and Freeman Gosden, who created and played the Negro characters, captured the ears of practically the entire nation every weekday evening at seven o'clock. Many families changed their dinner hours so as not to have any interference with the program. The telephone company discovered a marked drop in phone traffic each evening from seven to seven-thirty because people did not wish to make or receive any calls that would take them from their loudspeakers.

Family trips were delayed, vacations altered, homework postponed, discipline withheld, all so as not to miss a single episode of Amos and Andy. One morning the public woke up to discover that it would be possible to travel, to live among strangers in a public building and still not miss an episode of Amos and Andy. All they had to do was stop at a Statler Hotel.

The cost of radio equipment in the Boston house was $50,000 and it cost another $750,000 to wire all the rooms in Detroit, Cleveland, St. Louis, Buffalo and New York.

The Boston Statler opening was the grandest yet. Massachusetts Governor and Mrs. Fuller occupied the "Governor's Box" in the ballroom; Boston's newly elected Mayor and Mrs. Nichols led the Grand March. Bert Lowe and his 25-piece Statler orchestra played the season's popular dance tunes: *Varsity Drag, Singin' in the Rain, My Blue Heaven, Betty Coed, Ramona,* and *Three O'clock in the Morning.* There were souvenirs for each of the 3,000 guests — the men receiving a leather-backed clothes brush, the women a silver jewel box. Fox Movietone and Paramount News cameras photographed the arrival of the celebrities. The party lasted to dawn.

The following day, March 11, 1927, the *Boston Post's* lead headline on page one read:

STATLER OPENED IN SCENE OF SPLENDOR

The drop head read: *Huge Crowd Gathers Outside Hotel to Catch Glimpse of Big Festivities.* The second drop head carried the amazing information: *A Radio in Every Room!*

The story of the Statler opening received enormous press coverage from coast to coast and the other hotel men read it with dismay. A radio in every room! Statler had stolen a march on them once again. Just as a decade ago he had forced them to put baths in every room, he was now forcing them to put radios in every room. The costs would be staggering but they had no choice in the matter.

Slowly and grudgingly they began the installations but they were never really able to overcome Statler's competitive advantage. He was the pioneer, the first to provide free entertainment and the traveling public developed a Statler loyalty. His empire was to prosper and survive the Great Depression that was just coming over the horizon.

CHAPTER 32

"WE'D BETTER MAKE IT TODAY"

For a day that was to produce a significant event, April 30, 1927, began with a deceptive calm. The executive floor at the Pennsylvania Hotel was all but deserted that Saturday morning. There was a hotel trade association convention in Atlantic City and three of the Big Four (McKowne, Stoner and Hennessy) had gone there for the weekend. Statler was in his office but even he was being quiet. The sparks and alarums and excursions that usually issued forth were missing; he was in a mood strange for him — he was being contemplative.

The Boston house had now been open exactly 50 days and its success was clear. He had no immediate plans for building another hotel; he felt an unsureness about the future and didn't want to be over-extended if business didn't hold up. This was the time, he supposed, for him to transfer more management responsibility to his staff. In his mind he reviewed the strengths and shortcomings of each man, and concluded that he had as good a staff as was possible to put together. Besides, he'd be looking over their shoulders for some time to come and could correct any mistakes.

He put his hands behind his head and leaned back to stare at the ceiling, then at the opposite wall, finally at Alice Seidler who was typing some correspondence. Damn it, he thought, she *was* a slow typist.

"Miss Seidler," he said.

"Yes, Mr. Statler?" she swiveled her chair to face him.

"Miss Seidler," he repeated, "you know that you and I are going to be married some day. I think we'd better make it today."

As the color mounted her throat, he grinned happily. This was the first time he had been able to disconcert her.

After a long silence she spoke in a small voice. "It would be a great responsibility . . . with the children."

"They're my responsibility," he said.

"No, if we got married they would be both our responsibilities."

Those words seemed to ease a great weight he had long borne. He never would have married Alice Seidler merely to provide a mother; in fact he felt he should shield her from such entanglements and difficulties, but her determination to assume the job gave him great relief.

As for her, she was not really surprised at the sudden proposal. She had been aware of the not so subtle campaign among Statler's friends and associates to bring this about. When he had returned from Europe and expressed interest in the widow there was alarm among his friends and redoubled efforts to turn him toward Alice Seidler. Even the children, especially the oldest girl Marian, attempted to bring them together socially. More often than not Alice Seidler had turned down the invitations; she was not going to enter into any competition with the widow, or with anyone else. There were pride and dignity involved and, further, she was not at all certain she wanted to marry him.

Did she love him? Certainly not with the heedlessness of youth, not with those illusions of perfection, of perpetual bliss. For eleven years she had spent more hours per day with him than most wives ever do with husbands, and since he was not a man to dissemble she knew him thoroughly. What she felt for him was affection, compassion, admiration and pride. If that did not add up to the romantic concept of love, it was certainly a sound basis for marriage.

Also, they were both tired of working. Though they would not have admitted this fact to each other, perhaps not even to themselves, they had traveled a long road up from poverty and now they wanted to rest and enjoy the view. Surely they had earned the right.

The wedding took place that afternoon at the Fifth Avenue apartment of Franklin and Nell Matchette. Mayor Jimmy Walker had assigned a motor cycle cop to deliver a marriage license from the Municipal Building on Foley Square. At Alice Seidler's request the minister of the Fifth Avenue Presbyterian Church was present to perform the ceremony. Their hastily gathered attendants were her brother and his oldest daughter Marian.

In all the rush it would have been surprising if some detail had not been overlooked. It turned out to be a fairly important detail. The ceremony went smoothly until the minister was about to intone, "With this ring I thee wed." At that point Statler blushed and began to shuffle his feet.

"I forgot to get a ring," he whispered hoarsely to his almost–bride. The minister stopped and looked up with an expression that was part rebuke and part helplessness. Statler said, "Nell, can you lend us one?"

Nell Matchette nodded and went into the bedroom to rummage in a jewel case. She returned with a plain gold band and the ceremony proceeded without further hitch.

After the ceremonial kiss, the bride called the groom by his first name for the first time. "Ellsworth," she said, "the very next thing you do, please buy me a wedding ring."

And he spoke her first name for the first time. "Yes, Alice," he said.

After receiving congratulations the bride and groom entered a taxi and headed downtown. Statler took her hand in his and leaned back with a sigh of contentment. "We're going to have a happy time together, Alice," he said. "There's a lot I want to show you. We'll spend the winters in Florida and take cruises on the *Miramar.* And Europe! You must see Rome . . . and England and France and the rest of the countries."

He fell silent and gazed out the window, wrapped in happy contemplation. "Hey!" he suddenly cried, jerking erect and snapping his fingers in excitement. "Let's go down to Atlantic City and surprise the boys!"

Atlantic City was where the hotel convention was being held. Her honeymoon would be largely spent in a smoke-filled hotel room while he talked shop with his colleagues. She didn't mind, however. She did not expect to remake him, and besides, the hotel business was her life, too.

The executives of the Statler chain were indeed surprised when the boss and his secretary turned up as man and wife. They were relieved, too, for this union meant there would be a continuity of management and policies. Alice Seidler had had a hand in building the empire; she would not now try to alter it.

Like most brides Alice Statler wanted a home of her own. She was tired of hotel living where nothing ever seemed personal or permanent. She would have preferred to live in a modest house but she recognized that that was impossible; her husband's position and his temperament demanded something big. He wanted to show her off, and he wanted to show off for her.

Before their marriage he had purchased the Long Island mansion owned by the radio comedian Ed Wynn, hoping to install his children there and keep them together as a family. Now that he was giving them a new mother as well, he had high hopes of belatedly establishing a solid home. Immediately upon returning from Atlantic City he took Alice and Louis Rorimer out to the estate to plan remodeling and redecoration.

E. M. STATLER

The house was a massive wooden structure that contained unexpected dormers, pendants and finials on wooden icicles, a Gothic eave, a Romanesque porte–cochere. It borrowed bits and pieces of a dozen architectural styles, and if it had any genre of its own it could only be called "Long Island Rich."

Yet the total effect was not unpleasant. The wood had weathered to a mellow silver-grey, and surrounding the house was four acres of flower beds and groomed lawn that led down to the waterfront and the boat and bath houses.

Statler led his wife and his decorator through the house at a rapid pace, his eyes dancing with excitement. "Alice, you can have anything done to the house you want. Anything! Louis, I think you'd better add a new wing. I'd like a billiard room and you can put additional servants' quarters above it. And put an organ in the front hall, arranging the pipes up around the staircase. The boathouse should be enlarged; I have the *Miramar* and Milton is sure to have another boat or two and I want them under cover. Better build a greenhouse, don't you think, Alice? I'd like to grow some orchids. Perhaps you should have the landscape people put in a putting green. I'd like Alice to learn golf. And, Louis, I want you to go to Europe and get the best antiques to furnish this place. Get anything my wife wants . . . anything!"

They lived in the Great Neck house through the summer as the alterations took place. Alice hired the staff, which consisted of a housekeeper, a cook, butler, upstairs maid, downstairs maid, chauffeur, gardener and the gentle Anna Boyer who continued as governess to the two younger children.

If this was more display than Alice Statler really wanted, she understood it for what it was, an offering from her husband. She would not deny him the pleasure. Nor was it out of step with the times — this was 1927, the most

224

flamboyant year of all the Roaring Twenties. Jimmy Walker ruled New York, Al Capone ruled Chicago, Douglas Fairbanks and Mary Pickford ruled Hollywood — all with varying degrees of cynicism and drama. Lindbergh had flown the Atlantic, opening the heady prospect of regular passenger flights to Europe. A Frenchman, Emil Coué, had brought to America a self-mesmerizing chant that was on everyone's lips — "Day by day in every way I'm getting better and better."

Also, day by day everyone was getting richer and richer — on paper. Playing the stock market on margin had become a national craze and butchers and bakers aspired to mansions of their own. At least the money Statler was spending was hard money, earned the hard way.

It was late that summer that loss again hit Statler; his daughter Marian came home from Europe to die in the big house.

Marian, gentle Marian, had been her father's love. He could confide in her, secure in the knowledge that she would not censure him, or even judge him. The special feeling he had for this child was due, in part, because she was the delicate, the wounded one. She had been seven years old when he adopted her, a cripple. She couldn't walk (from polio) but had a brightness and sweetness of aspect that completely captivated Statler. He hired a physical therapist to attend her and was somehow able to imbue her with his own determination and courage. When she was ten she walked — not with tentative steps but with a stride of grace and certainty.

He called her "Chummy" and she called him "Daddy." When she was twenty-one he sent her to Europe. Within weeks she returned home and fell ill. It was pneumonia at first, then she died of an embolism. Almost at once the sunshine was gone and the chill winds of fall swept over the Sound.

Alice and Ellsworth packed up for Florida, going to

Fort Myers where several retired hotel men lived. Over the coming months Statler was to return twice to New York, but during neither visit did he go to Great Neck. He was never to see his house again.

During that winter the Statler public relations department arranged for a unique radio program to be called "The Statler Hotels Hook-up." The newly organized National Broadcasting Company was to broadcast an hour of music originating in the Statler Hotels in New York, Boston, Buffalo, Cleveland, Detroit and St. Louis. Each hotel was to supply two orchestras, the house dance band and a classical string quartet — a program of twelve orchestras in six cities. Statler himself was to come up from Florida to be on the show and make the opening and closing remarks. During the rehearsal he read his lines in his clear, high voice, then concluded by saying into the mike, "Goodnight, sweet Alice."

The program announcer, Graham McNamee, said, "Mr. Statler, you're supposed to say just what's on the paper."

"Oh?" Statler said with sweet innocence. He removed his fountain pen from his vest pocket, uncapped it, and wrote on the bottom of his script the words "Goodnight, sweet Alice."

McNamee frowned. "What I mean, sir, is that you are not allowed to make any personal greetings over the air."

"Who is not going to allow me?"

"It's NBC policy."

"Well, son, you go tell NBC to change its policy."

Within an hour the announcer was back with an NBC vice president who said, placatingly, "*We* have no objections to your saying goodnight to your wife, Mr. Statler, but it's a rule laid down by the FRC."

"Who is the FRC?" Statler asked.

"The Federal Radio Commission."

"You just go ask the FRC to make an exception this time."

"Oh, we couldn't do that."

"You couldn't, huh?"

"No, sir."

Statler thought for a moment, then said, "Well, now, either I say goodnight to my wife or you're gonna broadcast one hour of silence."

The program went on the air as scheduled, and at the close of it a vast audience heard Statler say, "Goodnight, sweet Alice." No reprimand came out of Washington. One would guess that the Federal Radio Commission (later named Federal Communications Commission) was too unsure of its own new powers to take on the peppery hotel man.

After the broadcast Statler returned to Florida to play bridge and golf and sit in the sun while he planned the great European tour on which he would take Alice. Old friends and associates who saw him this winter remarked on how well he looked, and how happy. He was learning how to play, and discovering that he liked it. He was gradually getting rid of the guilt feelings that had previously assailed him when he did not put in a full day's work.

It is likely that he could not have made the adjustments if it had not been for Alice. Like Statler, she had known work since childhood, but unlike him, her interests had not been confined to the hotel business. She helped him to see and feel and explore the wonders of the world that lay about them. She helped him to turn his curiosity outward from hotels, made him share her excitement of discovery. It was the most fortunate of marriages.

It had been their plan to return to New York in the late spring and from there sail for Europe. It was not to be. Statler was summoned north during the first week in

March to face a most unpleasant lawsuit. When he and Alice arrived in town there was a wet and bone-chilling wind sweeping through the canyons of Manhattan and he shivered when it hit him. He frowned with annoyance and wondered if he'd gone soft under the Florida sun.

They occupied their old suite at the Pennsylvania and he began conferring with his lawyers. The year before he had chartered his boat *Miramar* to a man in Miami. With the boat went the crew, a captain, several sailors and a steward-cook. The boat left Long Island and headed south for Miami, but instead of taking the inland waterway, the captain took her on the shorter, direct route out at sea.

Three days out and a violent tropical storm hit the *Miramar*. Sixty miles off Morehead City, Florida, she went down with all hands. Because she was on charter, Statler had no legal responsibility for the deaths of the crewmen, but he took on the responsibility nevertheless. He gave the son of the captain an executive job in his Boston hotel; he offered to put the children of the other crewmen through college; widows were offered cash or pensions. Despite his blamelessness and his generosity, several of the families joined together to sue him for several million dollars. Their actions both angered and saddened Statler, and indirectly led to his death.

CHAPTER 33

"I'VE APPRECIATED YOUR FRIENDSHIP"

On April 2, Dr. Nagel, the Pennsylvania house physician, invited the Statlers down to his Greenwich Village apartment for dinner. That afternoon Statler said to his wife, "I don't think I'll go to Nagel's for dinner. I'm tired."

She looked at him in some alarm. In all the years she had known him she had never heard him admit to being tired. She said, "I'll telephone them and cancel out."

"No, Alice, I want you to go. Mrs. Nagel has probably gone to a lot of work on the dinner and she shouldn't be disappointed."

After dinner with the Nagels, Alice told her host of Statler's admission to tiredness and the doctor was sufficiently concerned to return to the hotel with her. They found Statler propped up in bed, studying some business papers. He scoffed at Nagel for coming out in the middle of the night just because of some "sniffles," but he submitted to an examination with uncharacteristic docility. Nagel listened to his chest, thumped his back, looked down his throat, took his temperature, counted his pulse, then said, "You have a bad cold."

"Ha!" Statler snorted in derision. "You spent six years in medical school to tell me what I already know?"

"It's nasty weather for a cold. I want you to stay in bed tomorrow, at least until I look in on you."

"Ha!" Statler said ambiguously.

Nagel took Alice with him out in the hall where he said,

"A cold is nothing to fool around with. What we must guard against is pneumonia. He has so much scar tissue on his body that his skin can't breathe properly and he'd have great difficulty fighting pneumonia."

The following morning Statler made no attempt to get out of bed and when Nagel arrived he made no jokes about his condition. By the end of the week Nagel decided to call in another doctor for consultation. Together they reached the feared diagnosis — pneumonia!

It was the middle of the following week that Statler decided he was dying. One by one he called his friends and associates to his bedside. Dr. W. F. Randolph, the dentist with offices in the hotel, was among the first to be called, and his brief interview with Statler was typical of all that were to follow.

Statler took his hand briefly and said, "It's a damn shame, Randolph, but you and I have got to part our friendship." When the dentist began to protest, Statler waved him to silence. "No, no! I know the facts. I didn't want to leave without telling you how much I've appreciated your friendship. Goodbye."

So it went with each man summoned; a brief greeting, a quick goodbye; no commiseration, no sentimentality. He was managing his dying as he had managed his life, with brisk efficiency. Yet he seemed unable to mention his dying to Alice. Day by day she sat at his bedside, watching him grow weaker, but no words passed between them except the most cheerful. Occasionally she caught him studying her and she guessed he was trying to formulate a goodbye. Though she tried to help him, she too shrank from the finality. They remained mute about the love they felt for each other, each trying to spare the other the pain of parting.

At last, on the evening of April 14, he put his hand briefly on hers and said, "Alice, dear, go get a pencil and paper. There are some things I would like you to take down."

She ran down the corridor to the office, snatched up a secretary's dictation book and a sharp pencil, then ran back again. When she reentered his bedroom she found him in a coma.

He never regained consciousness. He died 48 hours later, the night of April 16, 1928. She never knew what his last words for her were to be.

Statler's death was worldwide news, as were the terms of his will. He left over a million dollars each to his three surviving children; hotel stock worth close to four million dollars was divided between his surviving sister Lillian, his surviving brothers William and Osceola, and Frank McKowne; substantial bequests went to his five nephews and nieces.

Ten thousand shares of Statler common stock (then worth $10 dollars) was marked to set up a Statler Foundation for the purpose of " . . . research work for the benefit of the (hotel) industry . . . training and making more proficient the workers in the hotels, for the benefit of the industry as a whole." — *Buffalo Times*, May 18, 1928.

The residuary of the estate (the amount was never publicly revealed) went to the widow who was made Chairman of the Board of Hotels Statler Company, Inc. The event was headlined:

> Hotels Valued at $30,000,000 run by Woman . . . Mrs. Statler is now, at 45, head of a . . . business said to be the richest corporation in the world controlled by a woman. — New York *World*

> Designation of Founder's Widow Makes Her World Figure as Public Hostess. — New York *Herald Tribune*

> . . . probably the most important woman executive in the world. —New York *Sun*

From that day forward Alice Statler's every act was done under the white-hot stare of the press. She endured this invasion, this inevitable result of wealth and power, with the same quiet dignity with which she had met poverty and obscurity. Her life had been one of extremes, neither of which altered or disoriented her.

Alice Statler remained active in the Statler management for the next 26 years, and when the chain was purchased by Conrad Hilton on October 27, 1954, it had almost doubled in size. Beside the founder-built hotels in Buffalo, Cleveland, St. Louis, Detroit, New York and Boston, Alice Statler's management had constructed, acquired or was in the process of building hotels in Washington, D. C., Dallas, Pittsburgh, Hartford and Los Angeles. Hilton paid $111,000,000 for the Statler assets in the largest transaction in the history of the hotel industry; in fact, the largest real estate transaction ever made.

Hilton went on to girdle the world with his hotels. It does not diminish him to say that he could never have known such remarkable success except for E. M. Statler, except for the pioneering, the visions and hard work of the uneducated glory hole boy from Wheeling.

The disposal of the hotels did not mean retirement for 71-year-old Alice Statler; it meant only that she was free to give full attention to what was closest to her heart, her job as Chairman of the Trustees of the Statler Foundation. She saw this as an instrument for the perpetuation of her husband's ideals. If Conrad Hilton could export the modern American hotel structure and technology, perhaps the Foundation could help (through education) to staff these hotels with men and women who would reflect the best tradition of American service.

The Foundation began to grant construction and scholarship money to high schools, trade schools and junior colleges for the teaching of labor skills in short supply (especially cooks and bakers), and to universities offering Bachelor of Science degrees in hotel administration. Since it had been the first university offering hotel courses, it was natural that Cornell should have received the greatest assistance. By 1966 the Statler Foundation had given the university more than $7,500,000 for the construction of teaching facilities, faculty salaries, research projects and student scholarships.

Cornell's Statler Hall was completed in 1950 and the annex, including the Alice Statler Auditorium, was opened in 1958. Together they house classrooms, laboratories, a library, and the Statler Inn — a university facility unique in all the world. It is a pilot hotel containing 36 guestrooms and baths, the proper public rooms, restaurant and banquet hall. Here the students learn engineering, housekeeping, purchasing, food and beverage management, and the myriad other details of hotel keeping including that ineffable but all important one of making the guest feel welcome.

Dr. Howard B. Meek, who founded the school, has retired, but his successor, Dean Robert A. Beck, aided by the Statler Foundation, has continued the Meek and Statler tradition with aggressive skill and kept the school preeminent. Cornell has graduated over 3,000 students at the current rate of 400 a year, and they are eagerly sought by the expanding hotel and restaurant industry.

There was a time when Switzerland was the outstanding training ground for the world's hotel managers, maitre d's, and chefs, but Cornell has replaced it. In 1964 foreign students made up 12.9% of the undergraduate body. They came from Austria, Canada, Colombia, Cuba, Cyprus, Egypt, Finland, France, Germany, Great Britain, Greece, Hong Kong, India, Israel, Japan, Lebanon, Mexico, the Netherlands, Norway, Pakistan, the Philippines, Switzerland, Syria, Thailand, Trinidad and Venezuela.

Upon graduation, the foreign students do not generally look for jobs in the United States but return to their homelands with the newly acquired American techniques and attitudes.

Statler long took pride in the fact that hotels brought strangers together and let them know each other and shed their preconceptions and prejudices. It was his hope that this role would be effective in the international arena, bringing whole nations into acquaintance and friendship. Certainly the Cornell School of Hotel Administration is an increasingly active agent in this crosspollination. This is Statler's monument.

No less than her husband, Alice Statler has led a life of service. She was fortunate that in widowhood she escaped the melancholy of everything completed; fortunate, too, in her present knowledge that when she leaves, the work will be so organized and so endowed as to perpetuate itself.

Statler was a success in a number of ways: he surmounted pain and sorrow in a lively manner; he employed his capacities to their limits; he kept his pride sufficiently in check so that he was not blind to his own shortcomings and failures; he imposed his vision upon society and left it improved; and in the process he collected an inordinate amount of the world's riches. He was successful in an Emersonian sense — it came as a by-product to his concentration upon a private dream.

> *"Is there not a certain satisfaction in the fact that natural limits are set to the life of the individual, so that at its conclusion it may appear as a work of art?"*
>
> ALBERT EINSTEIN

BIBLIOGRAPHY

Atherson, Lewis. *Main Street on the Middle Border.* Indiana University Press, 1954.

Browder, Lesley Highes, Jr. *E. M. Statler, Hotel Man of the Half Century.* Thesis, Master of Arts, Cornell, 1959.

Henderson, Ernest. *The World of "Mr. Sheraton".* David McKay Co., New York, 1960.

Hilton, Conrad. *Be My Guest.* Prentice-Hall, Inc., Englewood Cliffs, New Jersey, 1957.

Jarman, Rufus. *A Bed for the Night.* Harper & Brothers, New York, 1952.

Lopez, Vincent. *Lopez Speaking.* The Citadel Press, New York, 1960.

Ludy, Robert B. *Historic Hotels of the World.* David McKay Co., New York, 1927.

Madden, Clarence. *The Advertising of Hotels.* Hotel Monthly Press, Chicago, 1935.

Ritz, Marie Louise. *Cesar Ritz.* J. B. Lippincott Co., Philadelphia, 1938.

Sullivan, Mark. *Our Times,* Volumes I, II, III, V. Charles Scribner's Sons, New York, 1932.

Williamson, Jefferson. *The American Hotel.* Alfred A. Knopf, New York, 1930.

Hotel Gazette:	August 4, 1923. pp. 10-11
	February 2, 1924. p. 14
	May 3, 1924. pp. 10 ff.
	September 4, 1926. p. 6
	November 19, 1927. p. 18
	May 5, 1928. p. 10
Hotel Monthly:	March 1960. p. 36
National Hotel Bulletin:	February 1924. p. 100
	June 30, 1925. p. 5

Southern Hotel Journal:	Supplement to March, 1950 issue.
National Hotel Review:	June 30, 1923. pp. 13-17
	June 5, 1924. pp. 3-4
	May 16, 1925. p. 29
	May 28, 1927. p. 7
Nation's Business:	June 1928. pp. 11-15
Hotel Management:	February 1922. Vol. I. pp. 5-7
	May 1922. pp. 170-172
	August 1923. Vol. IV. pp. 40 ff.
	July 1925-April 1928. Vol. VII-XII
	August 1927. Vol. XII. pp. 122 ff.
Hotel Reporter	
Hotel World:	June 9, 1923. pp. 7 ff.
	August 4, 1923. pp. 29-31
	October 2, 1926. pp. 22 ff.
	February 12, 1927. p. 14
	May 5, 1928. pp. 5-7
New York Times:	April 25, 1916 6:2
	December 17, 1916 5:7
	June 3, 1917 4:1
	May 3, 1922 4:3
	June 4, 1922 7:4-6
	December 22, 1925 10:4
	April 4, 1926 26:4
	July 8, 1926 5:2
	May 1, 1927 1:2
	January 30, 1928 25:6
	May 19, 1928 1:6
Architectural Forum:	April 1919. pp. 95-108
	July 1923. pp. 11 ff.
Business Week:	May 7, 1955. p. 130
American Magazine:	April 1917
	May 1917
	June 1919

INDEX